Victory in Vietnam

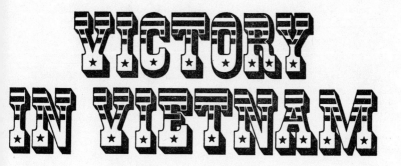

VICTORY IN VIETNAM

Richard West

Photographs by Philip Jones Griffiths

A Private Eye Book with André Deutsch

Published in 1974 by Private Eye Productions Limited,
34 Greek Street, London W1
In association with André Deutsch Limited,
105 Great Russell Street, London WC1

© 1974 Private Eye
© 1974 Photographs, Philip Jones Griffiths

Designed by Peter Windett
Printed by A. Wheaton & Co., Exeter
SBN 233 96611 0

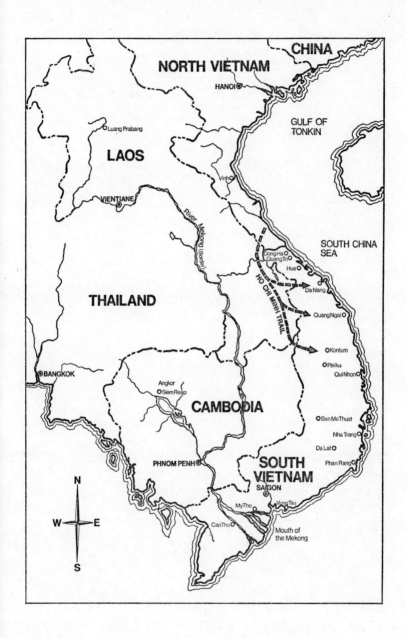

Preface

In January 1973 I was leafing through various magazines in a Scottish public library when I saw my own name in a puzzling context. It appeared that *Books and Bookmen* had asked the novelist Kingsley Amis to list the ten imaginary books that he would least like to read in the coming year. Knowing that Amis has always been pro-American, I was not too surprised to see that he headed his list with *West of Hanoi. A Sentimental Journey* by Richard West. I do not know whether Mr Amis has read my previous book *Sketches from Vietnam* (Cape, 1968, with drawings by Gerald Scarfe) but surely he could not have known that I did indeed plan a successor?

When I had finished *Sketches* in May 1967, I left Saigon with the idea that I would not return. But I was back by the end of the year, made two visits in 1968, two in 1969, 1970 and 1971. I was to have gone back in 1972 but for a ban on my entry, imposed at the request of the United States Embassy. On some of these visits I was employed and financed by a newspaper; on others I merely stopped off in Vietnam before or after working in nearby countries. It is a cheap country to live in, except for the Vietnamese, and one that I find unendingly attractive. On most of these visits I travelled about, kept a diary, and studied the country and its history.

In August 1973 I had two pieces of good fortune such as rarely coincide in the life of a free-lance writer: I was offered a free return flight to Singapore, and the Saigon government agreed to give me a visa. On 1st September I left for Vietnam with the vague intention of writing some newspaper articles but soon became possessed again with the idea of doing a book. I studied my notes and diaries from the previous visits, I roughed out a scheme of chapters and found a way of express-

ing what I had wanted to say. It could be and will be argued
that there is no place for another book on Vietnam, for another
stone to be heaped on that mountainous cairn of memoir and
argument. To which I can only reply that no book I have
read on the subject corresponds to my own opinion, still less
to my own experience.

This book is in part a reportage of Vietnam after the 'ceasefire' and the departure of the Americans; in part a reflective
study on the American role in the war; in part a personal
memoir of how I responded to Vietnam over eight years of war.
This is in no way a sequel to *Sketches from Vietnam* although I
have borrowed the same device of division by geography. The
first and final chapters are set in Saigon, the second in Hue
and the north-east coast, the third in the Central Highlands, the
fourth in the Mekong Delta and the fifth in Laos and Cambodia,
the two neighbouring states that have become so sadly em-
broiled in the tragedy of Vietnam. Throughout the book I have
tried to put the events of Vietnam in the other dimension of
history, to show how little was really new, how the events of the
Seventies had a precedent in at least ten decades beforehand. Although therefore this is not a history, it is not journalism, which
tries to present each new excitement as having no precedent in
the past.

Some of this material first appeared in the *New Statesman*,
The Listener, *Private Eye* and the *Sunday Times Magazine*, but
my last four-month visit to Vietnam was devoted exclusively
to this book and did not result in a newspaper article.

At first I thought of using the title suggested by Kingsley
Amis, but feared that it might contravene the Trades Description Act, since I have not been to Hanoi. The present title
imposed itself as I found that the illusion of victory is widespread in Vietnam, whilst Conrad's ironically named novel
Victory crops up in the first and last chapters, concerning the
death of two friends, Peter Duval Smith and Jean Ottavj.

It is to them that I dedicate this book.

Part One
SAIGON

1

At the end of my last book on Vietnam I described, shortly, the death of an unnamed British journalist in February 1967. This was Peter Duval Smith, a man whose manner of life and death were so strange and outrageous that I did not dare write more about him for fear of distressing his relatives. Since then seven years have passed, during which both his divorced first wife and his widow have been remarried so I am going to begin this present book where I left off, with Peter's death. I do so in no spirit of ghoulishness but because Peter deserved a longer obituary than he got from the London newspapers, and also because his exotic bitter romanticism reflected the character of the country in which he died. 'He liked Vietnam' could well have been used as his epitaph.

A few years after Peter's death the British Broadcasting Corporation published a book of some of his radio talks, which gave an idea of his zest for the outlandish and of his restless need for excitement. About his early life I know only what he told me, that he was born in Tanganyika in 1926, went to college in South Africa—his homeland—then earned a living by teaching and writing in Cairo, Athens and Hong Kong. When I met him first, about 1963, he had already made a name for himself as a radio commentator and reporter, coupled with rare but excellent essays in written journalism. I am told that he did some TV films on literary men such as W. H. Auden, but these I never saw. He seems to have been well known in intellectual circles in London and New York but I think he enjoyed himself more in the wilder parts of the world, especially Bolivia, Ethiopia, Ghana, Poland, Ireland and Vietnam.

Scandalous stories succeeded every journey. There was the piano thrown out of a window in Finland; the sexual inter-course with a pilotess high over Malaysia, during which the plane got out of control; the obsession with a tattooed girl in an Addis Ababa brothel. His first wife, Jill Neville, wrote a bitter novel about his drunkenness and his thoughtlessness, but he was also often a trial to less intimate friends. The writer Olivia Manning, at whose house Peter lodged for a time, said 'I didn't really object when the cleaning woman came into the room to find him masturbating; I did object to the fact that he didn't *stop* when she came in.' Drink and sexual excess may have contributed to the heart condition from which he died, but did not impair his energy and his curiosity. He was obscene, he shouted in public places, but while he could stand up he could usually say something interesting. His pale, spectacled face was always peering about for some new thing to examine or new person to talk with. 'My idea of heaven,' he told me once, 'is jumping out of a plane on a tropical airport—jumping because it's the sort of place that can't afford any steps.'

Peter came to the Far East on this last journey, having convinced the *Weekend Telegraph* that he could find ways to reach the 91st Regiment of the Kuomintang, a remnant of the Chinese Nationalist Army that had survived by running an opium trade in the mountainous borderland between Burma and Thailand. Many journalists had attempted in vain to reach this camp of bandits who prudently shot at over-inquisitive strangers, but Peter claimed to have found a Singapore Chinese who would furnish him with a *laissez-passer*. 'The story began,' he wrote in the posthumous article, 'drinking brandy at nine o'clock in the morning with a general.' So many mornings began that way with Peter that some of his friends feared he would never get down to work. But this general, over the brandy breakfast, gave the required letter to Peter, who then went to Bangkok to prepare the journey.

When I met him there, in December 1966, he was characteristically booked into two hotels, the Erawan for appearance, and a Petchburi Road motel where he could take his girls. It was the first time that I had met Peter abroad and, even knowing his London ways, I was taken aback by his vivacity. After a few beers, over which he discussed Conrad,* he wanted to visit a girlie bar recommended by a Dane. Here he picked up his first girl of the day and took her off to the motel in a taxi. When we met a few hours later Peter wanted to go to a massage parlour, so we sought out one that had not yet been overrun by American troops on leave from Vietnam.

'Do the girls here make love?' Peter immediately asked the fat Chinese manager, who replied with a coy simper: 'Maybe, if they like you'. Maybe was not good enough for Peter, who set off down the corridor, stopping to look into every cubicle through the peepholes installed to check on the behaviour of the patrons. The manager waddled behind, clucking his tongue and pulling at Peter's sleeve and begging him not to disturb the customers. I suggested we drank some beer before having a massage but Peter then noticed the two-way mirror through which you could see to choose your masseuse. Each girl wore a smock with her number on it, and I saw with surprise that Peter chose No. 12, a stocky peasant type, rather than one more delicate.

When the masseuse begins work she takes off her smock but

* He talked in particular of Conrad's *Victory*, the story of Heyst, a Swedish count who ran off with a girl from a women's English orchestra on tour of the Dutch East Indies. Conrad wrote: 'Heyst was not conscious of either friends or of enemies. It was the very essence of his life to be a solitary achievement, accomplished not by hermit-like withdrawal with its silence and immobility, but by a system of restless wandering, by the detachment of an impermanent dweller amongst changing scenes. In this scheme he had perceived the means of passing through life without suffering and almost without a single care in the world—invulnerable because illusive'.

keeps on a two-piece bathing dress, or at any rate that is the principle, but from Peter's cubicle there were soon sounds of struggle, a few squeaks of complaint and then hoarse grunts of lust. (Peter enjoyed noise, especially in sexual intercourse. He told me once of his excitement at having a Catholic girl on a jangling brass bed surrounded by pictures of the Madonna.) After the massage parlour we went to a blue film cinema, where most of the patrons looked furtive, but not, of course, Peter. He ordered beer and when the projectionist put on a new colour movie from Tokyo, he called instead for *Millie and the Dentist*, a ludicrous pre-war work, whose heroine looked about fifty and whose anxious, balding hero could not get an erection. After the movies Peter borrowed a few bahts and went off to the Petchburi Road.

When I saw him again in Saigon, about two months later, Peter seemed pleased with himself and his work. He had achieved his mission to find the Kuomintang regiment; he had escaped death from a drunken Thai soldier who fired through his car door; and here in Vietnam he had just had an exhilarating day in a small plane spotting for an artillery strike. I think he was one of those people who really enjoy danger, although he had the excuse of writing a book on techniques of modern warfare.

It was then two days before Tet, the Vietnamese New Year, which fell that year on 9 February. As usual during this festival, the government had relaxed the curfew laws so that the public could wander about, to shop and amuse themselves, all day and night for three days. They could also drink all night, as Peter discovered with fatal result. On the night of 7 February we set out for a long walk through Saigon, which to Peter appeared as a wonderland. He stopped at the food stalls to poke his nose into bowls of crab-meat and vermicelli, he rummaged through trays of herbal medicines, black-market tinned turkey and marijuana cigarettes, he questioned and talked with pedlars, shoe-shine boys, bar girls, hotel clerks and

Vietnamese soldiers. With Philip Jones Griffiths, the Welsh photographer, we ate at a Vietnamese restaurant—strong food, for Peter liked spiced small birds, pond fish and dishes of almost pure garlic. He got up once during the meal to demonstrate how a doctor giving a plague injection has to take a run-up before shoving in the needle. I am told that he was still on the spree until four in the morning when, having grown melancholy, he compared himself to Heyst in Conrad's *Victory*.*

The next morning, Vietnamese New Year's Eve, Peter appeared to have got back his cheerfulness. I saw him in Nguyen Thiep street hurrying in the direction of Tu Do as if he had some urgent appointment, but when I greeted him he explained that he always had to walk at top speed or he forgot where he was going. We went for breakfast at Brodard's café, a few yards down, where Peter began on a loud but quite funny imitation of an American journalist, followed by an equally loud imitation, with physical demonstration, of a breakfast taken with Graham Greene. According to Peter, the novelist suffered a bit from tremor. 'At this breakfast we both had terrible hangovers. Greene said that the best cure was coffee, a bun and a vodka. He ordered for both of us, but somehow he did something wrong. He shoved the bun into his mouth by mistake and then threw a glass of vodka over me—he was trying to hand it to me, you see.' I asked if Peter never felt shaky. 'No,' he replied, 'I merely suffer inside.' I heard afterwards that he was getting bad pains in the chest.

Later that evening I saw Peter with Mary McCarthy, the novelist, and Bernard Fall, the historian, who was killed a few days later by a land mine. Peter was trying to persuade Miss McCarthy to come with him to the opium den, which it had not taken him long to discover. She grinned amiably but pleaded another engagement. When I saw Peter next, at eleven

*'Ah, Davidson, woe to the man whose heart has not learned while young to hope, to love—and to put its trust in life!'

o'clock in the evening, he sat crouched on a bar stool at the Royal Hotel, looking very pale and tired. I told him to go to bed but he wanted to visit a certain pagoda to see in the Year of the Goat. The goat in Vietnam, as in Europe, enjoys a reputation for randiness, and Peter had great hopes of its astrological influence. I do not know whether he reached the pagoda but the last person who saw him alive, one of the hotel porters, said that Peter got back at 3.45, having to get up the stairs on all fours or by propping himself against the wall. The following afternoon, when he had not appeared for an appointment, we opened the door of his room to find him still dressed and kneeling over the end of the bed—like Livingstone at prayer in the Children's Encyclopedia, as someone later remarked. 'He's been like that all day,' said the room boy. The dark flush on one side of the face suggested death by heart failure.

Because of the New Year holiday it was difficult to telephone to the appropriate authorities and when we did get through, it was hard to hear because of the racket outside from firecrackers and thunderflashes. After about an hour a British doctor arrived to certify Peter dead and a British official arrived to register the same fact. It was not until late afternoon that the state officials arrived in the persons of 15 Vietnamese policemen, five US military police, including representatives of the Criminal Investigation Department, followed by five ambulance men and a well-known preposterous US colonel who had some responsibility for the foreign press. Everyone stood about in the dark narrow corridor waiting for the police inspector, a squat, scowling man, who gave his cigar stub to an aide to be extinguished then marched into Peter's room, followed by most of the multitude. For the first time I realised that this case was being treated as death in suspicious circumstances.

The body was photographed, the room repeatedly searched and all possible witnesses questioned. Outstanding of these was Jean Ottavj, the ancient Corsican owner of the hotel, who had long been a fine friend to us visiting journalists. When the police inspector asked if Peter brought women into his room M. Ottavj's big lower lip actually wobbled with indignation. 'No, never! These gentlemen are English journalists, very correct men (*très sérieux*)!' This statement, made by Peter's corpse, was startling and not quite accurate. Quite a few of the Royal guests brought back prostitutes; indeed one American unit trust salesman, with bracelets on both his ankles, once brought back four to the room he shared with his eighteen-year-old son. The English journalists, as befits serious men, may have been cautious of prostitutes for fear of being infected or robbed, but they could bring back girl friends. If M. Ottavj chanced to meet one of these girls on the stairs he always greeted her as 'Madame', ignoring the fact that these wives were subject to changes of height, face, hair, colour of eyes, and even of race. Moreover, from what I had seen in Bangkok, I did for a while suspect that Peter might have brought home some tough whore who had smashed him over the head and made off with his wallet. This theory was reinforced by the discovery that there was almost no money in the room; but even this fact was in character, since Peter was usually waiting for funds. The murder theory was ruled out when the porter confirmed in private what he had told the police in public, that Peter had come home alone.

Next it was suggested that Peter had died of drugs. A certain journalist said within earshot of the inspector (who luckily knew little English) that Peter had died from smoking bad opium brought in from Laos by a British TV producer—whom he named. A few days later the story went round that a half-empty syringe of morphine or heroin had been found in Peter's cupboard where, apparently, it had escaped several searches. I cannot imagine what the inspector made of all this, but he asked four of us journalists to appear next week.

By evening the argument over the cause of death had turned to an argument over what to do with the body. Somebody had telephoned the American press centre and asked for a '17th Field Ambulance' to take the corpse to the military morgue at the airport, but when the US colonel heard about this he flew into a fury and threatened to have the MPs turn the ambulance back into town. 'It'll have to go to the Vietnamese first,' somebody wailed, and one of the British consular men, who had been trying out the stretcher, said: 'There's no room at the embassy, and the air-conditioning isn't on over the holiday.'

I cannot remember where the body was kept until the autopsy (which showed ordinary heart failure, unconnected with drugs) for by then an argument had begun over the funeral arrangements. Peter had been a free-lance journalist, working for anyone who would pay him, but his main assignment in Vietnam had been for the *Weekend Telegraph*. The *Telegraph* organisation prides itself on its care for employees, but obviously felt that Peter did not deserve quite as much as a full-time journalist who had spent his life serving the paper. Anxious cables were sent from the London office to the *Telegraph* man in Saigon, requesting to know the approximate cost of bringing the body to London. The reply went back that Peter and coffin would cost the equivalent of two first-class aeroplane seats. What, cabled back London, were the possibilities of cremation in Vietnam? Okay and cheap, came the reply from Saigon, but first it would be necessary to get the widow's permission. WIDOW'S CONSENT RECEIVED, answered London, expressing as much relief as can be expressed in this electronic language.

Two days after Peter's death, I and three other journalists went to the police inspector who kept us waiting a long time but then had no questions to ask us. Everything was over except the cremation service, but even here a problem cropped up. The Saigon crematorium, as it turned out, was in territory still partly controlled by Communists and it would not be possible for the mourners to go there except under military escort. The cost of this, which might have had to be borne by the *Telegraph*, was out of the question, so Peter's body went to the flames unattended. Later there was a short memorial service at Saigon's Huguenot church, which would have touched him not because he believed, but because some of his Boer ancestors had been Protestant refugees from France. He must have been one of the first people to die in Vietnam's Year of the Goat.

2

In February 1967, when Peter Duval Smith died, the word Tet was known only to Vietnamese and a few foreign specialists. In January 1968 the whole world was amazed by the Tet Offensive, in which Communist troops, taking advantage of the holiday, seized more than half the countryside and several towns. They held the US Embassy in Saigon for only a few hours but hung on in Hue for more than a month.

Afterwards both sides claimed victory. The Communists said that the Tet Offensive had exposed the feebleness of US military power and so alarmed the American public that President Johnson had to stand down as candidate in the forthcoming elections. The American military claimed that the Communists suffered crippling losses, failed to make any lasting territorial gains, and got no response to their call for a popular uprising. There may be truth in both arguments, but I make no pretence to military expertise. I can only report what I saw of the effect on South Vietnam of this escalation of war.

At the time of the Tet Offensive I was in Eastern Europe, engaged on a cold and unprofitable journalistic assignment. From the Yugoslav and Bulgarian newspapers it seemed as though Communist tanks were rolling all over the country, that MIGs had mastery of the air and that Saigon was soon to be renamed Ho Chi Minh City. I wanted to get back. No newspaper was willing to send me but I did get an assignment in Kenya, which is on the way, with the guarantee of another job in Cambodia in the summer. By early April I was in Hong Kong, writing the article about Kenya, and three days later I was in

Saigon, then on a tour of the Vietnamese provinces. I was in Dalat on Sunday 8 May when the Communists launched yet another major offensive, once more overrunning part of Saigon, so I hitched a lift back to the city on a Presidential aeroplane which survived a few shots on approach.

Arriving at the Royal Hotel I found my colleagues in shock. Four British and Australian journalists had been shot dead that morning while travelling in their jeep to a contested part of the city. According to a survivor, who had played possum, the journalists had yelled 'Bao Chi' ('press') to the Communist officer, who merely laughed and then gunned them down. The US Ambassador issued a statement condemning the killings as an atrocity, but most of us regarded them as a mishap. It is unreasonable to expect that Communists in a battle should be able to tell the difference between military and civilian white men, especially since so many journalists carried arms. A representative of the grandest American newspaper had been seen to storm the Citadel at Hue, and in Saigon, during the May Offensive, a US photographer borrowed an M-16 to 'avenge a dead buddy' and was himself shot dead at the old French cemetery. In all, seven journalists were killed in Saigon that week.

There was a curfew for all but a couple of hours a day, during which M. Ottavj would hobble off with his stick to buy food and wine for his customers. As usual in time of confusion and fear, M. Ottavj and the Royal Hotel represented order and confidence. Dinner was served in the small *salle à manger*, separated by iron lace from the large room in which the entire staff and all their families were lodged throughout the emergency. As we ate in the evenings dozens of children in white pyjamas would stare at us shyly through the partition.

At seven next morning Philip Jones Griffiths knocked on my door and asked if I wanted to go with him to the area of fighting. He looked like a dog, with a walking stick in its mouth, that is eager to go for a run. Normally I stay clear of all forms of battle, especially since I have never worked for a newspaper that offered the two things—money and fame—that compensate a reporter for the risks he takes. My only outlet for articles at this time was *The Listener*; and who would lay down his life for *The Listener*? But although most battles are boring as well as frightening, a war fought actually in a city would, I thought, be interesting.

The Communists at this time held much of the south-west part of Saigon and its sister-city, the Chinatown of Cholon. The two sides were installed on either side of the Saigon Canal, which is crossed at one point by the Y-Bridge, known formerly as the Bridge of Love. An island in the canal, also reachable from the bridge, was supposedly neutral territory. From the Royal Hotel to the Y-Bridge took only ten minutes by taxi, in spite of the thousands of refugees who were crowding the streets.

Near the Y-Bridge Philip and I joined a platoon of the Vietnamese Rangers who were going to make a sweep through a suburb that had first been occupied by the Communists then shelled and rocketed by the Americans. All civilians were ordered to leave the district, which had therefore become a 'free-fire' zone, meaning that anyone who moved there was presumed to be a Communist. The patrol set off in leisurely fashion, taking advantage of cover along each side of the street. An army cameraman joined at one point and two days later I was to see on TV the very patrol at which I had been present; it looked very much more exciting—like one of those Westerns where Gary Cooper stalks villains through a deserted town. Behind the patrol came a van to collect the enemy casualties, who, whether alive or dead, were picked up by the arms and legs and hurled one on top of the other into the back. One of the dead carried a pretty if rather blood-stained ammunition pouch in the VC colours, which I removed (and later gave to a German Communist girl), but unfortunately one of the Rangers spotted me and immediately started to re-examine the corpses to find what loot he had been missing. Another Ranger, enrolled as a mascot, was a boy of ten or eleven, with blood-thirsty small-talk. 'Yesterday I kill mother-fucking VC-ess. No shit!' Some said that this VC-ess, or female VC, was the little boy's own mother, but nevertheless he was publicised in the government press as a symbol of youthful patriotism.

At one point during this slow progression I became detached from the rest of the platoon and was startled to hear a voice behind me say '*Bonjour monsieur*'. A neatly-dressed, elderly Vietnamese had come up a side street to warn me. '*Attention*! There are two VC in the house opposite'. As I gaped at him, he continued by asking if I would do him the honour of visiting him at his home down the street.' 'But you're not supposed to be here', I said, 'you could be bombed.' '*Monsieur*,' he retorted with pride, 'it would take more than these events to move me out of my house.' He invited me in, poured me a large whisky (very welcome that morning) and showed me photographs of his career as an NCO in the French army. 'Fifteen years' service, *monsieur*, and if it was left to me I could clear these Communists out in a day'. However it was noticeable that his family and the neighbour, whom he had bullied into staying, were far less confident than this fierce old soldier and kept on asking me what the situation was. Rather bewildered by this incident, as well as by the heat and the whisky, I thought I had better rejoin the patrol before I got lost in a deserted city. The old soldier took me back to the corner where the VC were, and I saw the patrol in the distance.

Not all the casualties here were VC, and Philip took some grim photographs of children killed by shelling and rockets from helicopters. The carnage had been especially bad on the island in the canal, which houses one of Saigon's largest municipal slaughterhouses. On the first day of the offensive many people had fled the Communist zone to get away from the bombardment and had settled as refugees in the cattle pens and pig sties, from which they could see their houses burning only a few hundred yards away. However, the VC had briefly come to the island; it therefore became a free-fire zone, even though the bombardment took place after the VC had left. The whole place stank of dead humans and animals and was loud with the noise of air strikes on the other side. Philip and I detached ourselves from the patrol and he warned me that we might be attacked by the refugees if they thought we were Americans—the people they blamed for the attacks. I said we were French, a more familiar people than the English, whereupon we were greeted with smiles and even invited to eat meals cooked in the stalls and sties.

I thought at the time that there must be some novelty of the macabre about a battle fought in a slaughterhouse but, as so often in Vietnam, it had all happened before. A year or two after the May Offensive I read George Rosie's intriguing book on *The British in Vietnam*, describing the little-known and disastrous occupation in 1945, when by arming Japanese prisoners and letting the French loose to attack the anti-colonial Vietnamese, Britain touched off the war that has now lasted nearly thirty years. The Vietnamese politicians, who had been attacked in their offices in the Saigon Town Hall, called for guerilla war against the British. They were poorly armed but managed to put up a fight in some districts, and as Rosie reveals, one of the bloodiest battles, between Vietnamese and Indian Army troops, took place at this very same slaughterhouse on the island in the canal.

The carnage in 1945 was slight by comparison to the May Offensive, for only fighting men were affected. From the Y-Bridge in 1968 one could see the full folly and cruelty of unleashing remote, technological war onto a city. About 200 yards away a helicopter was firing rockets down into a large building, a factory that was said to contain VC. Flames were leaping up, to cheers from the Y-Bridge, when a Vietnamese policeman approached us and said there were no VC and that some of his own colleagues were in the factory. Nobody paid any attention and indeed there seemed to be no officer or responsible person present.

An American TV crew had been filming the refugees who kept retreating over the bridge, but the producer obviously thought that the film was lacking excitement, for he grabbed a US soldier and pointed towards a building about 100 yards away. 'VC!' he yelled, 'look there!' 'Where, where?' asked the soldier, so the producer took his carbine and pointed it for him. 'Oh yeah,' said the soldier. Still not convinced, he squeezed off a few rounds and soon other soldiers were firing at roughly the same target, which turned out to be stables in which some civilians were sheltering. A few horses and people may have been killed, but the TV crew got some memorable footage.

The only admirable people on this occasion were the Buddhist monks, who ventured deep into Communist-held districts to bring out wounded civilians. Foreigners used to sneer at these young Buddhist 'boy scouts' (I did in *Sketches from Vietnam*) but there was no doubt of their courage on the Y-Bridge. One could not say the same of the US troops from the infamous 9th Division, which had already wrought such destruction in the Delta but proved unwilling to fight for the Vietnamese capital. They skulked most of the time behind their tanks, whose turrets carried Confederate flags and whose insides were crammed with looted drink and miniature TV sets. It was in 1968 that one first began to detect the collapse of morale in the US Army.

3

The collapse of morale in the US forces was one of the most important yet puzzling phenomena of the Vietnam war. As late as 1967 most of the troops one met were disciplined, patriotic and willing to fight—in short 'motivated', to use the American jargon. By 1970 a good part of the army was drugged, depressed, unwilling to fight, and its patriotism was undermined by black and radical extremists. Some of this change may be attributed to the failure to win the war, although, since most of the dissidents were enlisted men serving only one year, they could not plead battle fatigue or war-weariness. Nor were the symptoms of demoralisation, especially drugs and radical politics, restricted to the troops in Vietnam; they were fashionable at the same time in the United States, or 'the world' as it was called by the troops. It may be that these fads in America were in part a reaction to the war—I cannot pretend to judge, and in any case I am concerned with Americans only in so far as they concern Vietnam, (too many American books about Vietnam are really about America) and wish only to point out that this collapse of morale, so gleefully chronicled in the liberal press, also had some effects and implications that ought to trouble the liberal conscience. But first I must attempt an analysis of how and when the rot set in.

Looking back at my diaries for 1966, I am astonished to recollect the mood of the US army. Here for example is an infantry lieutenant talking about a battle in a rubber plantation near An Loc. 'You hear people say how proud they are of their troops and you think it's all bullshit, but I felt like crying fifty times yesterday . . . You can't ask for better citizens. They're going against everything that's natural, doing their job. I can't get over some of my people, I mean a guy apologising for leaving, someone coming up and thanking me.' Here he stopped and blew his nose. Before the subsequent funeral service he asked that a rifle and bayonet should be stuck into the earth to mark the men who had died, a plan that was squashed by the sergeant owing to shortage of bayonets. This lieutenant, the sergeant and most of his platoon talked with a patriotism and sense of duty reminiscent of Hollywood films of the Second World War.

And so it was with the most famous regiment, the US Marines, whose battle song used to be known to every American child:

From the halls of Montezuma to the shores of Tripolee
We have fought our country's battles on the land and on the
sea;
First to fight for right and freedom and to keep our honour
clean,
We are proud to bear the title of the United States Marine.

The marines won further glory storming Pacific islands during the Second World War and it was natural that they should be first to land in South Vietnam in 1965. Their rigorous, even harsh training had instilled in them total obedience to their officers; if they were told to attack, they attacked, but if they were told to be kind to civilians they just as readily helped to repair huts and to give injections to pigs as part of a 'civil action' programme. But at Tet 1968 even the proud US Marine Corps lost its nerve and had to be replaced in the First Corps area by its hated rival, the First Air Cavalry; and the blow to morale from the Tet and May offensives was still more crushing to ordinary infantry divisions, some of which had to be split up and merged into the Americal Division, which perpetrated the My Lai massacre.

During the next three years it was impossible not to notice the signs of increasing discontent—the peace badges stuck into helmets, the sentries goggle-eyed on grass, the Negro troops with their black power salutes, their Afro haircuts and saucer-shaped dark glasses, comprising an army within an army.

One of the many underground newspapers that opened in army units actually called on its readers to murder their colonel; and a whole *quartier* of Saigon was taken over by US deserters, who posted permanent sentries to warn against the arrival of the Military Police.

The progress of demoralisation has been recorded for future historians in the files of a most unusual newspaper, the *Overseas Weekly*, Pacific Edition, which was edited for its first five years in Saigon by a pretty young woman, Ann Bryan. The *Overseas Weekly* started in Germany after the Second World War as a newspaper for the troops, but unlike the semi-official *Stars and Stripes* it had no respect for the authorities and much offended the Pentagon by revealing that one general had handed out right-wing John Birch society leaflets to his division. From 1966, when the *Overseas Weekly* began its Pacific edition, it was banned by a majority of the PX (or army) stores and had to be sold in the streets or by subscription.

Its news stories, especially its reports of court martials, were factual and stark, as were its inquiries conducted among the troops. 'Troops throw Frag (*fragmentation*) Grenade at Lt. Colonel,' said one typical headline (5 May 1969), or 'Angry G.I. guns down Captain with M.16' (24 July 1971). An *Overseas Weekly* investigation (3 January 1972) showed that in the three years ending in 1971 there had been 500 cases of 'fragging' assaults with grenades or other explosive devices, most of them against officers or senior NCO's. 'From the Delta to northern I Corps,' the *Overseas Weekly* reported, 'fragging in Vietnam has become a way of life'. The court martial reports also describe attacks on civilians, for instance a bar girl, Miss Anh.

'We sat there about fifteen minutes, then there was a shooting. Miss Anh was shot with a small gun. After he bought her tea, he says: "Are you shitting me?" Then he shot her'.

The *Overseas Weekly* reported but did not comment upon the growing use of drugs towards the end of the Sixties. In one survey (23 August 1969) a soldier is quoted as saying: 'If it weren't for Mary Jane here I would have gone completely out of my mind'. And next week the same reporter observed: 'Many G.I.s feel that compared to the world, Vietnam is a head's paradise because of the relatively low price of grass and lax attitude towards pot users by the military.' The *Overseas Weekly* also recorded the increased use of stronger drugs, ranging from speed, through opium to heroin.

It is an article of faith for the self-styled 'love generation'— the long-haired, Rolling Stone, macrobiotic-dieting, Woodstock, non-verbalising, sometimes infuriating followers of a fad which spread from California to most of the western world—that marijuana and other drugs induce a spirit of peace. For this reason they welcomed the news that eighty per cent of the troops in Vietnam had at least tried 'Mary Jane'. Fellow-journalists in Saigon, most of them years ahead of the 'love generation', refused even to argue the possibility that drugs could induce aggression, in spite of historical evidence that, from Indonesia to Morocco, hashish or bhang or marijuana was commonly taken by soldiers before battle, making them fearless and pitiless. There is evidence to suggest that drugs had the same effect in Vietnam.

The military authorities of course claimed that marijuana made men more inclined to violence. An *Overseas Weekly* article under the strong headline 'Why do our troops shoot each other?' (20 June 1970) quoted an army doctor as saying that opium and racial tension were partly responsible for the fact that forty or fifty per cent of gun-shot wounds were inflicted on GIs by other GIs. The view of an army doctor might be discounted but even a small sample of *Overseas*

Weekly articles shows evidence to support this. One man interviewed had grown paranoid from marijuana, thinking that everyone was a Communist and trying to kill him. 'I even thought the dogs in the compound were communists. They kept looking at me with their eyes. I thought about killing myself because I didn't want to be captured alive by the Chinese.' Here is the court martial report on two men who murdered a local civilian: 'Slicksleaves Kenneth E. Ritter and George English puffed on pot but they were far from relaxed. In fact they wanted a little action. The two troopers from the 335th Trans. Co. decided their idea of sport would be to go out and harass some Vietnamese people' (8 February 1969). If gentle people who smoke pot become more gentle, is it unreasonable to suppose that brutes who smoke pot become more brutal?

At the trials of Calley and others for the massacre at My Lai, it was stated in evidence that many if not most of the men responsible had been smoking marijuana not long before the shooting began. I do not suggest that the massacre took place simply because of drugs but that massacres are likely to take place when an army's discipline and morale have been broken so that the death of one soldier from stepping upon a Viet Cong mine panicks the rest into wholesale killing of villagers. There is a good comparison with the German Wehrmacht during the Second World War. The disciplined, crack troops who scored the victories in the early part of the war were well behaved, even friendly towards the conquered civilians. The massacres of whole villages in France, north Italy and Eastern Europe were committed either by para-military groups like the SS and the Gestapo or by frightened, untrained and ill-disciplined old men and boys who had been dragged into the army towards the end of the war. Similarly a Vietnamese villager in a contested district had less to fear from the earlier Marines than from the later army of radicals, Black Panthers and drug addicts.

4

One of the sadder casualties of the Vietnam war was the comedian Bob Hope, who suffered there an injury to his pride, his professional reputation and perhaps even his faith in America. The occasion, which I shall later describe, was a concert given at Long Binh on Christmas Day 1971, when a large part of the GI audience made a political protest against Hope and the US government. The event was the more extraordinary since Hope is not just an actor but an American institution, a leading Republican, a friend of Nixon and Agnew, a multi-millionaire, an impassioned anti-Communist, in short a patriot, perhaps all the more so since he is English-born. Each Christmas season since 1942, Hope had taken a troupe of performers abroad to entertain the GIs in places ranging from Germany to Korea, from Guantanamo naval base, Cuba, to the strategic air force base in Greenland. In 1965 he went for the first time to Vietnam, where the risk of mortar attacks from the never far-distant enemy added an extra anxiety to the routine hardships of road-shows. In recent years all the Hope Christmas shows had been filmed and edited for a highly successful TV film, so in a sense these tours had a professional nature, but there was no doubt of Hope's genuine sympathy and respect for young, lonely and fearful soldiers. Yet in 1971 some of them gave him the raspberry.

The spectacle was especially poignant for those like me, who had been brought up on Bob Hope jokes and had thought of him as the archetype of the better kind of American. As a radio comic during the Forties he specialised in the sort of dirty joke that now sounds infantile but seemed to us prurient schoolboys the very limit in daring and wit. Nobody quite knew which jokes he had actually uttered, or merely had attributed to him, but this was the level of humour: 'Did you hear about the little girl who swallowed a pin but didn't feel the prick till she was sixteen?' To a repressed generation Hope seemed an iconoclast, a speaker of unspeakable thoughts, almost a rebel. His reputation increased with a number of films, some of which, like the 'Road' series and *Paleface*, were genuinely and enduringly hilarious. The character played by Hope in these films was the All-American Man turned inside-out, the coward pretending to be the cowboy hero, the he-man who never gets his woman, the weak guy disguised as the tough guy. What might be described as the Texan ethos has never been better mocked than in one great scene from the *Road to Utopia*, in which Hope and Bing Crosby are dudes seeking their fortune from the Alaskan gold rush. Mistaken for dangerous gunmen, they act out their parts by swaggering into a miners' bar where Hope first reassures the customers that they are 'not in a killing mood today—only a wounding mood' then inadvertently orders a lemonade instead of a whisky. Seeing the incredulity on the barman's face, he adds with a snarl: 'In a dirty glass.'

But Hope the iconoclast proved to be Hope the priest who really believed in those all-American virtues at which he had once seemed to sneer. The purveyor of saucy jokes now entertained at the White House; the friend of GI's had turned into a branch of the Pentagon. My first sight of this new Bob Hope, so different from the comedian on the screen, was in December 1968 when a newspaper thought it had got permission for me to accompany the comedian on his Christmas tour. I went to Bankgok, from which Hope was to fly each day to Vietnam, and booked into the Erawan Hotel, where Hope and his troupe would be staying. I waited three days, growing crazed by the hotel's one tape of piped Christmas music, endlessly tinkling 'Tannenbaum,' 'White Christmas' and

'Rudolf the Red-nosed Reindeer'. Then at 6.45 on 21 December a lady press agent rang up to my room to say that Hope and the 75-strong supporting cast had arrived last night. 'It's real great to have you along and I think we're going to have a real fine time,' she prophesied, wrongly as it turned out, for I had not received proper permission to travel aboard Hope's plane.

The downstairs part of the Erawan had been overrun by the Bob Hope troupe of starlets, musicians, public relations men and two sombre Jews, rendered melancholy by their jobs as gag-writers. On the fourth floor there was a military 'Bob Hope Room' staffed by a colonel, seven junior officers, several sergeants 'and of course a sergeant-major to make sure things get done,' the colonel told me, 'It's really like a Corps Joint Command in a very exciting operation. Mr Hope is really a wonderful person.' This was also the view of the lady press agent who told me: 'You don't need to introduce him anywhere. He's an institution like Home, God and the Queen.' There was great excitement about a rumour that North Korea might soon release the prisoners from the American naval vessel *Pueblo*. 'Just think,' said one of the Bob Hope troupe,'if the news came through during one of our shows. I don't want to sound mercenary, I'm just thinking what it would mean to those boys. Most of the show is geared to faces of the audience, all of them lonely for their wives, sweethearts and families.' This was true. The TV programme that is made from the shows gives much space to soldiers in the audience, often holding up placards proclaiming their name or their home town to ensure they are seen by their family and friends. It would be churlish to suggest that by including these shots the TV company guaranteed that their programmes was watched by almost everyone in the United States with a friend or relative in Vietnam and the other countries toured.

It was becoming clear that I and the photographer would not get permission to join Hope on the plane. The press in Vietnam

was the responsibility of JUSPAO (or Joint United States Public Affairs Office) but the plane and its passengers came **under** MACVEE (Military Allied Command in Vietnam). However, when the plane returned it became the responsibility of MACTHAI (the opposite number in Thailand). I pestered the Bob Hope Room, I pestered Bob Hope himself but learned that my position was 'a conditional negative'. Getting desperate at the thought of what my newspaper would say, I bearded Hope at a reception where he was talking to three generals who said, very patiently: 'We at MACTHAI have no co-ordinating authority with MACVEE that empowers us to take non-military personnel on an aircraft'. Bob Hope, who had been listening, muttered something out of the corner of his mouth.

So I spent that Christmas in Saigon, and it was not until Christmas Day 1971 that I got to see a Bob Hope show in Vietnam. It was held just east of Saigon, at Long Binh, where the Americans had their largest military installation outside the United States as well as the largest military prison. However the inmates of 'LBJ', as the jail became known in President Johnson's regime, were not in the 10,000-strong crowd that attended this Christmas Day show. We reporters who boarded the military bus to Long Binh were each given a purple identification pass showing Bob Hope's face and the inscription 'Operation Jingle Bells'. We were also promised packets of 'Christmas Candy, compliments of the US Navy,' but this had run out when it came to my turn. Spirits were low on the journey, for most of the few reporters had been to parties the night before, while Long Binh Motorway is a *via dolorosa* of truck depots, tyre dumps, rusting water tanks, hovel complexes, barbed-wire hedgerows and petrol stations of every oil company known to capitalism. On arriving at Long Binh we were shown into a room decorated with Air Force plaques—'Golden Hawkies, we cover the sky'—and posters explaining the perils of heroin. Before going out to the stadium, we were given quarts of Foremost Fruit Cup, then turkey sandwiches containing bones big as a sheep's.

The show started at 1.30. It had been due to start at one but most of the GI's in the audience had taken their seats as early as ten o'clock. After two hours of waiting under a shattering, dry-season sun the mood of the crowd was restless and ready to quarrel. The private soldiers sitting in stands on three sides of the stadium could not help but observe the comfortable fold-up chairs in front of the stage for the officers and their wives and their distinguished guests, who were greeted as they arrived with abuse and hissing. Any army is treated with indulgence on Christmas Day; but this was not any army. The remaining 160,000 troops, compared to the half million five years before, were no longer interested in what remained of the war and took pains to avoid any fighting. In the Long Binh area there had been rumours of fake charges to frame political radicals in the army as well as a drug raid on the outpost called 'Whisky Mountain'. Radical troops had been still further annoyed by the refusal of visas to Jane Fonda, the left-wing actress, and members of her theatre company, who had wanted to tour Vietnam with an anti-war play.

Some of the radical soldiers had set up a picket outside the stadium bearing signs like 'Peace Not Hope' and 'Where is Jane Fonda?' Inside the stadium many groups were making their feelings heard by exploiting the old convention, already mentioned, that films of the crowd would appear on TV. This year there were still some placards of greetings to folks at home —'Hello El Paso', 'Minnesota, We Like It Cool', or simply 'Hi Goodboro'—, but there were more and bigger banners of a political character: 'Help Keep Whisky Mountain Clean', 'Merry Christmas Nixon, Wish You Were Here' and 'We're Fonda, Hope', with crafty emphasis on the comma. Whenever a TV camera turned on the crowd it evoked a salutation of two-finger signs, black clenched fists or white arms stretched high for peace. After three and a half hours waiting under a sun that threatened to boil the brains in the skull, there were bursts of booing, slow hand-claps and jeers. To make things worse an officer started to make an idiotic announcement: 'In the event of a mortar or rocket attack, the personnel on the right . . .' The rest was lost in derisive laughter because everyone in the tightly packed audience knew that 'in the event of a mortar or rocket attack' there was nothing to do but pray.

The Bob Hope troupe this year included a line of chorus girls, a singer, a pair of roller-skaters and the actress Martha Ray. It should have included the reigning Miss World but this lady, a hot-tempered Brazilian, had fallen out with the contest promoters and had to be replaced by Brucene Smith, 'Miss World U.S.A.', a small-town Texan girl with acting talents to match. In deference to the black troops there was a black girl singing trio and Vida Blue, a black Californian baseball player who also served Hope as straight man in some of the comic dialogues. The band eschewed soul, rock or any music that might appeal to an audience under the age of forty. It sounded old-fashioned even to me.

It was Hope, especially in monologue, who set the pace of the show. He came on holding a golf club, and that was the last I saw of him, for my view of the stage was obscured by TV cameras, or to borrow the pithier phrase of the soldier sitting behind me: 'I can't see shit for goddam TV shit'. The view was still further obscured by the immense cue-boards, or 'idiot cards' from which Hope read off his jokes, although it must be said that he read them well. Unfortunately this show was near to the end of his Christmas tour so that I, and presumably most of the audience, knew most of the wittier jokes from reports on earlier shows in *Stars and Stripes*, the services newspaper. Some jokes were purportedly anti-officer—'There's so much brass here the GIs sleep to attention'—but few of the audience can have felt that Hope was on their side against the army establishment of which he was so clearly the darling. Hope sounded uneasy about his marijuana jokes, which had first been put in the script in 1969, but he got some laughs with his description of baseball as a game in which 'you can spend eight months of the year on grass without getting busted.'

The old Bob Hope radio show may have been daring and dirty, but since then Hope has become more prim; and society less prim. The GI's at Long Binh, raised in the age of 'Hair', 'Oh Calcutta!', the Woodstock Festival, wife-swapping clubs, the Gay Liberation Front, 'The Myth of the Female Orgasm' and TV full-frontal nudity, were understandably not aroused by this typical piece of dialogue.

Miss World America: 'What would you do if your girl friend asked you to pay for a new dress?'

Bob Hope: 'Talk her out of it.'

The jokes and the display of girls were meant to remind the soldiers that they were red-blooded, virile, heterosexual, hundred-per-cent Americans, whose only desire was to get back home and bed down a fine, big-busted, American girl. But did this audience want such assurance of its virility? There was a chilly, even embarrassed silence at two Hope jokes about homosexuals; this generation, unlike the last, is not emotionally fearful of dissidents in society. The same silence greeted Hope's jokes against women's lib. There was something almost obscene and flesh-creeping about this elderly man who kept nudging the ribs of the young. There came to my mind the harsh words spoken by Prince Hal to Falstaff, 'How ill white hairs become a fool and jester.'

Yet it was not his age that divided Hope from his audience because, so I had read in the *Stars and Stripes*, the favourite comedian of the radical young was the long dead W. C. Fields. But Fields, or at least the Fields we see on the screen, was not the kind of man who becomes a multi-millionaire, the friend of Nixon and Agnew, least of all an apologist for America's role in Vietnam. It was not Hope's age but his politics that upset this Christmas Day audience. One joke really inflamed the crowd or, in the words of a radical in the stands, 'it had them

up on their feet shouting.' The joke as I noted it, was: 'You're
off the front page back home. The Vietnam War is now tucked
away between Lil Abner and Chuckle a Day.' It was like a dig
in the broken ribs. With one joke Hope had confirmed the two
most painful suspicions of most of the men in the audience, that
people back home did not appreciate them; and worse, that
although the war was as far as ever from being won, the news
of it was being played down to help Nixon win an election.
After this joke Hope was constantly heckled with shouts like
'Where's Jane Fonda?' Black militants rushed to the front to
wave their fists into the camera. A group of military policemen,
of all people, climbed onto the stage in front of Hope to unfurl
their banner: 'Pigs For Peace'.

Towards the end of the show, when a general came on stage to
thank Hope and to present him with a 'Ho Chi Minh bicycle',
scores of soldiers ostentatiously stood up and walked out of
the stadium. Clearly rattled, Hope shouted back at the hecklers:
'In my heart, you're the guys that are against war because you're
the guys that are helping to end it. You've all listened to that
garbage of the other cats . . . What have they ever done for
the world? They talk a lot about the My Lai massacre but that's
a load of nothing because they forget the good that we've done
helping little kids and building orphanages . . .' The actress
Martha Ray joined in the attack on the opponents of the war:
'Those characters you hear about and read about, they couldn't
shine your boots and don't you forget that!' This brought a
round of applause from the loyalists in the audience but the
Negro sergeant beside me remarked: 'Get most of these kids
back home and they'd be doing the same thing they're clapping
against'.

After the show Hope held a press conference for the few
journalists who had stayed the length of the show. If he had
been upset by the demonstration, he was too good an old
trouper to show the fact. Instead he wanted to talk about his
improbable plan to go to Hanoi to negotiate for the release of

the US prisoners there. This time, Hope told us, he was willing to go to North Vietnam to give a show for the prisoners or even for Vietnamese children, but had not pressed the suggestion as it was rather too much to ask. I thought of the North Vietnamese children, watching that incomprehensible show by the citizens of the country that was bombing them, and I thought once more of the saying that had been current for more than a year and was reproduced on a banner by the picket outside Long Binh: 'The Vietnam War Is A Bob Hope Joke.'

5

One breakfast-time in the Royal Hotel we were being pestered as usual by shoe-shine boys who walk in from the street almost at will. But at least, said my English friend, they do the job thoroughly if you pay them. He had come back from the north the previous day and given his filthy boots to one of the crippled boys, who had spent an hour bringing them to an exquisite polish. My friend had been so impressed, and so reluctant to haggle, that he had paid the boy well over the odds, a magnificent fee. Just at this moment, about nine o'clock in the morning, my friend was dismayed at the sight of this shoe-shine boy staggering tipsily into the hotel. He crashed into a wall, fell double over the back of the chair but still managed to utter the cries of his trade: 'Number one shoe-shine! No sweat!' A waiter guided the boy back into the street and explained what was only too obvious to my friend and me, that yesterday's tip had been spent on today's dose of drug—possibly binoctale, a hallucinogenic, but more probably heroin.

When I first came to the country, opium-smoking was prevalent among older Vietnamese, and marijuana-smoking among the Americans, but there were almost no cases recorded of heroin abuse. Today opium addicts complain that they are starved of good-quality stuff; but heroin, made from an opium base, is available in abundance in its purest, most deadly form. The heroin epidemic that struck US servicemen early in 1970 received much publicity in America, which itself suffered an epidemic and feared the return of a new legion of addicts.

Few Americans know, or care, that after these last troops came home, the South Vietnamese suffered their own heroin epidemic, one of the worst of the many plagues that have ravaged this country. At the end of 1973 the South Vietnamese police offered the estimate that there were 130,000 heroin addicts, although some foreign drug experts would double that figure. The figure of 130,000 compares with 5,000 in Britain and 400,000 in the United States, a country ten times as populated as South Vietnam.

The figure is still more horrific when one considers that of these heroin addicts the overwhelming majority are young males in the cities, especially Saigon, where a fix or smoke of almost pure heroin is obtainable for about 50p. The first Vietnamese to adopt the heroin habit were often the shoe-shine boys, petty thieves, cigarette stall-holders and prostitutes, who had themselves 'pushed' the drug to American servicemen. These sub-proletarians were worst hit financially when the Americans went and frequently took to the drug as an antidote to hunger. In the bars, often quite empty of customers, the girls fight off their boredom and anxiety with binoctale pills that attack the nerves and may cause death in a few years, especially when taken with alcohol.

As in the United States, the drug wave has fostered a crime wave among addicts needing to pay for a fix; in turn the police have begun a campaign against the pushers, whose offence, in theory, is punishable by death. The government has established a drug clinic at Long Binh, where Bob Hope performed, and several private people have opened smaller clinics, two of which I visited and shall describe. But first it is necessary to recount at some length the history of the drug traffic here, and its part in the war. Much of my information comes from *The Politics of Heroin in Southeast Asia* by Alfred W. McCoy, whose study of published sources has been backed up by painstaking private research and interview.

The Vietnamese word *Ma Tuy*, meaning heroin, is sometimes

referred to ironically as MACVEE, after the US Military Assistance Command, which ran the war in Vietnam. The joke is a reference to the widespread belief in Vietnam that the heroin derives from American soldiers. It is McCoy's thesis, at first almost too dreadful to be accepted, that American agencies such as the CIA not only condoned but even promoted the heroin traffic, and are largely responsible for the epidemic in Vietnam, the neighbouring states and America itself. He argues, again with conviction, that the CIA's use of the heroin traffic to gain political ends has direct relationship to the use made of the opium traffic by former British and French imperialists. The politics of heroin in Southeast Asia cannot be divorced from the world-wide trade in the drug, so that any analysis of the problem must begin, where McCoy begins, in America and Europe.

Heroin, at the end of the Second World War, was no longer regarded as a dangerous social problem. It had first been sold commercially by a German firm, but when its addictive character was detected in America in the Twenties, the narcotics officials had cracked down on its sales. The drying-up of supplies during the Second World War meant that, in the United States at least, addicts had to endure an enforced 'cold turkey', or de-intoxication. The traffic in heroin to the United States was revived by two organisations, the Mafia, based in Sicily, and the Alliance Corse, of Corsicans based in Marseilles, both of whom understood its commercial possibilities. Both organisations, however, were then in a feeble condition, the Mafia having been crushed by Mussolini's Blackshirts and the Alliance Corse compromised by their connection with the Nazis. But both in Sicily and in Marseilles the Americans looked on these criminal organisations as useful allies against the Communists, who appeared as the premier enemy in the late Forties. The American Mafia boss, Lucky Luciano, was let out of prison and sent to Italy, where his thugs were enrolled against the left wing. In Marseilles the CIA set up a coalition of Corsican gangsters and right-wing socialists to break the power of the communist dock workers, who had placed an embargo on arms for Indo-China. Thus, in the Forties as in the Seventies, both Sicily and Marseilles played essential but different roles in the world heroin traffic. The Mafia, with their criminal organisation inside the United States, could build up and supply a network of addicts and pushers. The Corsicans in Marseilles were not only more skilled in the chemical job of refining heroin, but possessed an organisation in Laos and Vietnam, then French possessions, which were to become the world's major sources of opium and its illegal by-products.

Opium comes from the gum of the highland poppy which flourishes in the Asian mountains from Turkey, though India to northern Indo-China. Its charm as a narcotic was known from the start of history but its value as a commercial crop did not become known until the age of European imperialism. The British in India, in the first half of the nineteenth century, bought and sold opium for the local market, but also saw its potential for a broader political purpose. Anxious to open up China to British commerce, they first bribed and then coerced the Chinese to let the drug into their moribund empire. The result was the infamous Opium War, after which the defeated Chinese were drugged, demoralised and in the end crushed. In the European settlements on the coast millions of Chinese were allowed and even encouraged to soothe their unhappiness with the opium pipe, and as Chinese emigrants moved to Malaya, Thailand and Indo-China, they took the narcotic habit with them. The French in Indo-China, far from attempting to put down the drug, made it the cornerstone of their local economy. Only six months after annexing Saigon, in 1862, they imposed a franchise on opium brought in from India, taxed at ten per cent of its value. The Opium Monopoly was later reformed and expanded so that by 1918 there were 1,512 government dens and 3,098 retail shops. Thanks to opium, which provided one third of the revenue, Indo-China started to turn a profit.

Between the world wars, when other colonial powers tried to suppress this social evil, the French actually raised Indo-China's revenue from the opium tax.

Before the Second World War the French had regarded opium as just a source of revenue, but afterwards, in the fight against the Viet Minh, they learned its political value. Throughout Vietnam, but particularly in the south, the French could combat the Communists only by making alliances with minority groups such as the Catholics, the Cao Dai sect and above all the river pirates, called Binh Xuyen, after the village near Saigon which was their base. The Binh Xuyen, who had smashed the Communists in Saigon, were paid in part for their services by control of casinos and brothels, but they and the other mercenaries still needed money to fight a war that was given only reluctant support by the government in Paris. The legal traffic in opium, which had once given the colony one third of its revenue, had been abolished in 1946, but a clandestine traffic continued, and it was this that French intelligence agents first took over and then expanded into a business called 'Operation X'.

The opium for 'Operation X' was supplied from Laos and north-west Vietnam, where a French intelligence officer, Major Roger Trinquier, had built up an army of mercenaries from Meo and other tribespeople. This arrangement was doubly ingenious since the Meo mercenaries benefited from growing the opium, while the mercenaries in the south got the benefit of its sale. The middlemen in this operation were Corsican gangsters in Vientiane, from where it was flown south on military planes of the French intelligence service. In Saigon the raw opium was refined by the Binh Xuyen and sold in their opium dens, any surplus being exported to Marseilles, for further refinement to heroin.

'Operation X' was brought to an end by the French defeat at the hands of the Communists. The 40,000 mercenaries in the north failed to relieve Dien Bien Phu, and their leader Major

Trinquier started a new career, first as supervisor of torture in Algeria, then as a leader of Tshombe's mercenaries in the Congo. The French held on in South Vietnam until 1955, when they were pushed out by right-wing nationalists under the leadership of Ngo Dinh Diem. As a pious Catholic, Diem at first tried to suppress opium dens and with them the traffic, but he too was to find that he needed the money. His brother and chief of security, Ngo Dinh Nhu, wanted to keep down the Communists by the establishment of a huge police force, backed by hundreds of thousands of paid informants.* This police force, which would also be used to protect the Diem family's power, demanded immense and secret funds which could not go through the official state budget. Therefore Nhu in person approached the Corsican gangsters, who were eager to re-open business with the approval of the police, even if some of their profit had to be split. So from 1956 until 1963 there was an ever-increasing traffic in opium to Saigon, first on charter planes owned by Corsicans and later on Vietnamese Air Force planes commanded by Nguyen Cao Ky, a rising young officer. In Saigon Nhu's police extracted a big profit from selling opium to the dens and to individual addicts.

Like most police states, the Diem regime ran on a nation-wide system of bribery, nepotism and jobbery which much offended his high-minded American supporters. With the assistance of US Ambassador Cabot Lodge a military coup was arranged in which Diem and his brother were killed, to be replaced by a military council. During the subsequent period of uncertainty, in which various generals took part in a series of coups, the police system built up by the Diems broke down from want of the opium funds. This opened the way to the Communists, who from 1964 found it very much easier to enter Saigon, to organise cells, plant terrorist bombs and even to hold political rallies. The agents who once would have informed on them were no longer getting paid. The Communist infiltration

* There were to be 200,000 in Saigon alone.

and a series of startling bomb attacks alarmed the military council, which decided in 1965 to strengthen security under a tough prime minister. The man they appointed was no other than Nguyen Cao Ky, the former head of Air Transport Command, who once had run opium for the Diems. The new Prime Minister, who also commanded the air force, chose as head of security and police General Nguyen Ngoc Loan, later immortalised by the photograph of him shooting a VC prisoner.

Within months of coming to power in 1965, Ky and Loan had rebuilt a police system quite as efficient as Diem's, and indeed they re-employed many of Diem's officers and informants. They also set out to build a network of influence that would bring in money and guard them against rivals. Although Ky and Loan had little influence in the army, Thieu's base of power, they had the police, the air force and the airport customs, and they were to establish their men in the dock customs, the newly created parliament and the Army II Corps, whose highland region was useful for smuggling opium. For opium was, of course, to be Ky's basic income, supplemented by sales of offices and licences for bars, brothels and building, all of which were booming with the arrival of the Americans. On the other hand military graft from sale of promotions, robbing the peasants and stealing supplies, went largely into the coffers of the Thieu organisation.

Premier Ky had no difficulty in reorganising the opium trade. He had good connections in Laos, including the Corsican gangsters, the Lao aristocracy and his own sister, who ran a hotel at Pakse, a convenient staging post. The Laos government had disbanded the Corsican airlines, but a replacement was found in South Vietnamese transport planes which could run very freely between the two countries. Much of the opium was smuggled into Saigon airport while the rest was dropped in the Vietnamese highlands to be picked up by Ky's agents. Most of the opium was at first sold to local addicts, but a cutback of Turkish opium in this period brought an increased demand from Europe for morphine base to be turned into heroin. A former CIA colonel in Saigon told McCoy (p. 173): 'Loan organized the opium exports once more as a part of the system of corruption. He contacted the Corsicans and Chinese telling them they could begin to export Laos's opium from Saigon if they paid a fixed price to Ky's political organization.' The drugs were dispatched by ship from Saigon port, whose director during this period was Ky's new brother-in-law, Lt. Col. Pho Quoc Chu.

Unfortunately for Ky, the very success of his new organisation increased the jealousy of his main rival Thieu. When Thieu, in 1967, stood down from leadership of the military council and put himself up as candidate for the revived position of President, Ky agreed to stand as Vice-President but scarcely concealed his ill-will. The glum, hard-working Thieu, although less glamorous than his premier, had built up a network of influence in the all-important army; moreover he was thought more reliable by the Americans. After Thieu became President he slowly increased his power at the expense of Ky, whose organisation was still further damaged in mid-1968, when Loan was shot and disabled by Communist fire and six more cronies were killed by a US helicopter, which rocketed them in a not very convincing 'accident'.

Although Ky lost power and eventually his premiership, he retained his command at Saigon airport and with it a share of the drug-smuggling business. Most of this business however passed to President Thieu, who in turn appointed a ruthless and entrepreneurial chief of police, Dang Van Quang, who had once commanded the rich Mekong Delta area. At his head-quarters town of Can Tho in 1966 Quang had established a monopoly for his bar and I well remember the fury expressed by Americans at having to patronise his over-priced beer and girls. At the end of that year he was sacked for corruption—quite an achievement in South Vietnam—but recompensed with a job as Minister of Planning and Development. After Thieu's

v.v.—D

election as President in September 1967, Quang was appointed Special Assistant for Military and Security Affairs, the equivalent job to that held by Loan during the days of Ky. Gradually Ky's men were removed from office and six of them were removed from this world in the aforementioned rocket 'accident'. The Thieu apparatus also established control over the drug business, although new methods of transport had to be used since much of the air force remained in Ky's control. President Thieu's own service, the navy, was used to bring drugs from Thailand or to safeguard their import on fishing vessels; when the Vietnamese army went into Cambodia in 1970 drugs were brought back to Saigon by the supporting planes and helicopters,* and members of the House of Assembly favourable to Thieu were allowed to bring in contraband after their frequent trips abroad.

Yet a third political drug ring was formed in 1968 by Tran Thien Khiem, who in the following year succeeded Ky as Premier of Vietnam. A devious plotter and trimmer, Khiem had been brought back from exile by Thieu to be Minister of the Interior, a job he used to advance his grasping family. Relations or in-laws were appointed Director of Saigon Port, Deputy Governor-General of Saigon, Director-General of Police and, most charming of ironies, Chief of Customs Fraud Repression Division. This gentleman was to be described in a US Provost Marshal's report as 'a principal in the opium traffic who has an opium habit that costs approximately 10,000 piastres a day and visits a local opium den on a predictable schedule. He was charged with serious irregularities approximately two years ago, but by pay-offs and political influence managed to have the charges dropped. When he took his present position he was known to be nearly destitute but is now wealthy and supporting two or three wives.' Relations

---

* In December 1973 a US Customs official in Laos whose job is to stop the illegal narcotics traffic confirmed McCoy's thesis that most opium now goes to Vietnam via Cambodia.

between the President and the Premier have since become cool, but as I write this (in Saigon, December 1973) their rival narcotics rackets continue to prosper.

As the war carried on into the late Sixties and grew ever more unpopular with Americans, others besides the Provost Marshal began to inquire into the Indo-China drug trade. Questions were asked in Congress; articles appeared in the press; the commander of II Corps, although a favourite of the US Embassy, was sacked for his flagrant involvement in the drug trade. Yet the US government and its officers in Vietnam continued to play down this unsavoury subject. One obvious reason for this was the fear of embarrassing Thieu while his troops were fighting alongside the Americans against a common enemy. Another reason, less widely obvious at the time, was the role of American agencies in condoning and even abetting the growth of opium for the trade. We have seen already how French agents like Trinquier recruited Meo mercenaries and encouraged them to farm opium poppies. In those days the Meos were used as auxiliaries for the French troops fighting in north-west Vietnam. In the Sixties they were recruited and trained to harass the Communist line of supply, or 'Ho Chi Minh Trail' from North Vietnam, through Laos to South Vietnam. To please and to pay the Meos, American agents encouraged the cultivation of poppies, whose harvest of raw opium was carried to Vientiane, processed and sent on either to Thailand or South Vietnam. But the Meos controlled only one part of the 'golden triangle' in the mountainous region of Laos, Thailand and Burma. The rest was ruled and exploited by two other groups which were thought politically useful by the CIA. The less important of these were the Shans of North-east Burma, whose partially Christian people had long been in revolt against the socialist government in Rangoon. A more important and viciously rival force are the Kuomintang, a remnant of the Chinese Nationalist troops who had been driven south from their country by the victorious Communists.

In the early Fifties they were financed and paid by the Americans on condition they struck back into Yunnan Province to lead a popular rising. When the attack was repulsed and the rising failed to take place, the Americans still paid the Kuomintang for intelligence work against China. In return the Kuomintang troops got control of the world's largest supply of opium, providing as much as half of the illegal traffic. When Peter Duval Smith reached the Kuomintang he was told by their general, Tuan Shi-wen: 'Necessity knows no law. That is why we deal with opium. We have to continue to fight the evils of Communism, and to fight you must have an army, and an army must have guns, and to buy guns you must have money. In these mountains the only money is opium.'

The Americans, like the French before them and like the British in China in the previous century, excused this dirty traffic because it was necessary, and anyway opium was a harmless drug, and if it was not, well, it was smoked only by natives. What had been condoned became a scandal in 1970 when it was realised that opium from the 'golden triangle' was being turned into heroin and sold on a massive scale to US troops in Vietnam and even exported to North America. There had been cases of heroin use by GIs before, but it was not until 1970 that Vietnamese drugs rings started to push phials of heroin to the bored men, using a sales force of vagabond children, cleaning-women, marijuana stall-holders and ARVIN soldiers or officers. Within a year the prevalence of addiction had grown into a national scandal, featured on the covers of *Time* and *Newsweek*. Outrage increased when it was learned that senior Vietnamese officers were engaged in exporting heroin to Latin American ports for sale in the United States, the country that deserved something more for its help. Newly addicted GI's, who wanted to keep up the habit after their discharge in the United States, rivalled the ingenuity of professional smugglers in getting heroin home. Several consignments returned in the corpses of fallen soldiers.

Even after this scandal the US government persisted in playing down the importance of South-East Asia in the illegal heroin market. It risked an alliance to put the blame on Turkey, which does not provide even a tenth of the opium, compared to more than two-thirds from Burma, Laos and Thailand. For years America cried out against the traffic from Turkey, through Sicily and Marseilles, but ignored the larger business in countries like Laos and Vietnam, which were virtually under American government. For example USAID in Laos gave generously to finance a Pepsi Cola plant which for years did not produce a bottle because, so McCoy was told by the US Bureau of Narcotics and Dangerous Drugs, the plant was used as 'a cover for purchase of chemicals vital to the processing of heroin'.

The departure of the American troops deprived the Saigon government both of military protection and of a market for heroin. To make things worse, the US customs department tightened up control on the export of narcotics from South-East Asian ports.

The poppies have still been grown, the opium processed and the heroin brought to the cities; but now it is sold not to American troops or Corsican merchants, but to fellow Asians. Thailand, the Philippines and Hong Kong have serious social problems caused by the drug, but only in South Vietnam is there a heroin crisis so grave that the very President who has exploited the drug feels obliged to speak out against it. A law has been passed making the sale of drugs a capital crime, and drug-takers are thrown into prison without medical treatment. However voluntary patients can get some sort of care in the government clinic at Long Binh or in one of the many private clinics, largely financed by the rich parents of addicts but treating people from all social classes.

The first clinic I visited is appropriately near Saigon airport, where so much of the heroin arrives. It is named Mac Tin, after St Martin, and appropriately it is run by an unfrocked

Vietnamese priest. He was not present, but I was shown around by a younger priest, in gold-rimmed glasses, and by various teachers who double as warders. Of the two hundred boys in this unusual boarding school, almost all were committed on the instruction of their parents or by the authorities of the state schools from which they had played truant. Three quarters of them have limited freedom to study in class, to play and to eat in the dining hall but the newly committed addicts are locked up, about five to a cell, for the first few weeks from their arrival. 'The bad boys', I was told by one of the teachers, 'are kept in punishment cells where it is very hot in the afternoon'. He indicated a row of wooden doors that I had taken for lavatories, broom closets or clothes lockers. Then I noticed the gap at the base of a door through which a plate had been shoved and then a hand. Kneeling down, I saw that this 'bad boy' was staring out with one eye at the visitor speaking a foreign language. Those confined in the punishment cells may have been suffering painful withdrawal symptoms, or 'cold turkey', which we have seen on TV or read about in the newspapers. Yet, having known a few heroin addicts in London, I was surprised by the relative calm of these boys at Mac Tin. They smiled and joked from behind bars; there were no signs of the bitterness or affected remorse often found among captives. I may have been duped, but I did not spot signs of that acute 'cold turkey' of which the symptom is literally climbing up the wall. An attendant said that the boys were given a drug to help them over the worst days of withdrawal but he claimed that none of them had to spend more than a month in confinement. I know nothing of drugs and I distrust the conflicting experts, but it seems reasonable to accept the thesis that the Vietnamese addicts suffer less from withdrawal symptoms because they have taken a pure form of heroin.

The physical state of these boys at Mac Tin was far less gruesome than I had feared beforehand, but what one might call their spiritual state was doleful beyond description. The street arabs among them, much like the street arabs at liberty, kept going with jaunty stoicism; but those from middle class homes were depressed and depressing. They are custodians of the future in a country that has no future. Unless their parents are very rich they will serve about ten years in the armed forces, a prospect summed up by the tattoo (under the other needle marks) on one boy's arm: 'La Femme. L'Amour. La Mort'. And if there is no love, heroin. A nineteen-year-old called Nguyen said his parents had sent him here yesterday when they found he had gone back to heroin after six months in a prison clinic. He had been buying ten smokes a week at 500 piastres a time and when I asked how he had got the money, he grinned and repeated that he had been sent here by his parents. Presumably he had been robbing them. 'I smoke because my friends smoke,' he said. It is what almost all of them say and sounds just as reasonable as the same explanation given by boys in London for drinking beer or going to bed with a girl. Nguyen was alarming simply because he was not a neurotic, not a misfit, not in revolt against his father. I asked Nguyen and told him to ask the others in his cell what they hoped for in life and what they wanted to be. They conferred a moment, then Nguyen replied quietly: 'Nothing'. He was not striking an attitude of defiance, despair or self-pity, nor do I think that he was shy of talking to someone twice his age, for the Vietnamese have not swallowed the modish guff about a 'generation gap'. He and his friends took it for granted that I understood why they were heroin addicts; and knowing this country, I did.

The second clinic I visited, on the other side of Saigon, was dispiriting in a different way. It had begun ten years ago as a school for delinquents, or 'vagabonds', and was run on a harsh, even military system. The director Ho Quang Phuoc is an engineer, owning a rice mill in the Delta, who said that he started the school because he loves children. ('*J'aime les gosses*'.) At the time of my visit his boarders included three sons of generals, six of colonels and six of members of the

House of Assembly, but there were also many poor orphans whom he had taken in because he loves children. The boarders varied in age from boys of ten to a soldier of twenty-nine who said he had gone onto heroin because he had been deserted by the girl whose name is still tattoed on his chest. Most of the addicts here had been committed by their parents, whom Dr Phuoc blames for his unsuccessful cases. 'A heroin addict is cured in four stages of three months each,' he explained, 'but many parents think their boy is all right after the first stage. They take him out, he meets his old friend and he is back here by the end of the year.' I did not discover what kind of medical treatment is given to addicts but Dr Phuoc insists on their having a vegetarian diet, much of which is provided from the surrounding vegetable gardens, worked by the boys. 'We cut off the heroin from the start,' he said, 'which is worse for the boys who injected the drug than for those who smoked it. Generally it is the richer boys who smoke because it comes more expensive. The poor boys, the street urchins, can only afford to inject.'

I went on a tour of inspection that must have been pre-arranged, for as each class sprang to attention, the nearest boy would be brought forward for interview. 'He is a half-caste by a French father', said Dr Phuoc, '. . . . he is a half-caste by an American father'. Both these children looked miserable and embarrassed, and I did not want to talk to them in the presence of Dr Phuoc, let alone their class-mates. We went to a shed by the vegetable garden to find some fifty very young boys paraded in ranks in front of a prefect of twelve, who ordered them about in a voice grown prematurely hoarse. 'One, two, three, four', and the class started to mark time, clump, clump, clump, clump, the short bandy legs rising and falling, the bare feet turned outwards, slapping the concrete, smack, smack, smack, smack. The prefect started to sing and the boys joined in 'Clementine', but I did not enjoy the music nor the sight of those shifty and sullen faces. After marking time for a while, the boys were marched off in columns around the room singing their national anthem: 'Vietnam, Vietnam,' clump, clump, 'Vietnam, Vietnam,' smack, smack. When it was over the staff clapped their appreciation.

'Vietnam, Vietnam . . .' A few days later I asked a Vietnamese lady to give me the words of the first verse of the national anthem. 'Nobody knows them,' she said. 'The anthem was written by a musician who is now a senior leader of the National Liberation Front. The government kept the music but it commissioned new words. But nobody knows them or cares about it.' It must have been hard to compose verses in praise of a country whose young are sold heroin by the chief of police, the present and former prime ministers and the President of the Republic.

Part Two
NORTH

I used to think of the east coast airports as stations of the cross on the road to the Golgotha of the de-militarised zone. Qui Nhon, Quang Ngai, Danang, Phu Bai (serving Hue), Quang Tri and Dong Ha had little of cheer to offer. Today Dong Ha and the Demilitarised Zone are in Communist hands, while Quang Tri is a frontier town—and also, almost incredibly, a tourist attraction, since the Saigon government encourages foreigners to observe the city won back at such cost by its army in 1972. Last year, 1973, I went first to Qui Nhon and Danang, two major sea-ports where in the past I had spent some of the nastiest weeks of my life. In the time of the Americans it was in these two towns and the nearby countryside that one saw most starkly the degradation and suffering caused by the war.

Qui Nhon

The province of Binh Dinh, of which Qui Nhon is the capital, has reasons to be the most hate-ridden in Vietnam. It has been a Communist stronghold since before the Second World War and, during the late Sixties it was policed by South Korean troops. The Korean 'psy-op' propagandists and some of the more gullible journalists believed that 'Asian speaking to Asian' could pacify the province. In fact the Vietnamese so hated these fellow Asians, as much for their black market activities as for their cruelty, that when South Korea played football against Australia in a knock-out match in Saigon, the

51

crowd cheered on the white men. It is true that the ruthlessness of the Koreans achieved a sullen peace among most of the peasants, driving the rest into refugee camps in Qui Nhon, but in 1972 almost the whole province went communist, including the districts once shown to me by the Koreans as triumphs of their 'psy-op'.

When I went to Qui Nhon in 1966 and again in 1969 it had seemed to have all the unpleasantness of Vietnam in the utmost degree—the filthiest refugee camp, the smelliest slums, the most dust and barbed wire, even the most dangerous airport, cradled by high hills. 'I'm taking her in to land,' the pilot had yelled on my second flight to Qui Nhon, 'but I don't think we're going to make it.' The hinterland was mangy from defoliation and pitted with bomb craters; a nurse at the British children's hospital said that even the toddlers, when asked how they got their wounds, pointed skywards and said 'B-52'. Apart from the island of Phu Quoc there was no place in Vietnam in which I had so strong a sense of being hated as a foreigner. This hatred was returned in full by the South Koreans and, after they left, the Americans. One American in Qui Nhon, a lugubrious construction worker, said to me once: 'There's a captain I know here who's done two tours of duty and he regards this country with passionate hatred, I mean hatred. He's really worked at it. He says, and I've got to kind of agree with him, that the only solution to this country is to withdraw all the Americans and then to plaster the whole goddam place with nukes. Then after it was all over he'd take up an airplane with two monkeys, a male and a female, attached to two parachutes. And just before throwing them out of the plane he'd say: "This time, don't fuck it up!" I told this story to my wife—she's Vietnamese—and she got really mad . . .' He seemed pained by the recollection. 'To call a Vietnamese a monkey is worse than calling him a "dingaling" or "dinki-dau". If you called one of those women out there in the street a monkey she'd really kill you.' Thinking about his wife made the

construction worker still more glum. 'She'd previously lived
with a captain then with a sergeant. I bought a house for her
mother but not for the rest of her relatives when at the same
time they were looking down their noses at her for working in
a bar. She was uneducated so I gave her money to study
English and typing so she'd be able to get along without me
if she wanted. That was my big mistake. When I wanted to
take her away with me to Taiwan, she decided against it and
disappeared.'

Now it is the Americans who have disappeared, and I
noticed that even the children have lost those phrases of
English they used to shout at the passing white man: 'Hey you!'
'Number One!' 'You give me!' 'Okay Salem!'* Now they
shouted in Vietnamese, except when some older child with a
more retentive memory remembered the yells of yesteryear.
One of the few Americans that I saw in Qui Nhon was a
merchant seaman who told me: 'We're probably the last
American ship that will ever come here. We're taking away
ammunition cases and also some of the generators we gave
these people during the war.' He talked of the war as though
it was over, as indeed it was for the Americans. 'I used to come
here regularly with a troop ship for the Koreans, bringing in
the new recruits and taking away the veterans. I guess the
Koreans weren't very popular here, but neither were we. I
guess there's nobody sorry to see us go'.

Well, almost nobody, but I did get to know one person who
mourned the Americans. She was about thirty, rather plump for
a Vietnamese and she kept a café remarkable for its one

---

* 'Okay Salem!' was the cry most often heard in the 'time of the Americans'. I once worked out a scholarly and elaborate theory that 'Salem'
derived from the same roots as the Hebrew 'Shalom' and the Arabic
'Salaam', both greetings that mean 'peace'. From there I went on to suggest
that the Vietnamese were of semitic origins, possibly one of the lost tribes
of Israel. Unfortunately for my theory, 'Salem' clearly derived from the
unpleasant American cigarette of that name which the children wanted to
cadge.

decoration. This was a blown-up photograph (which I saw several times later) of a beautiful Vietnamese girl with her hair hanging down over one eye and a big tear rolling down from the other. On her left hand, carefully lighted, one saw her wedding ring, and from the right hand there dangled a soldier's identification disc. The proprietress saw me staring at this and explained: 'She widow, same-same me. My husband go into army ten years ago. He die.' Later she had been 'married' to an American and had earned good money, first as a PX salesgirl and later at Jimmy's Bar in Qui Nhon. She had borne him a son, who now, at six, stood taller than his sister three years older. When the Americans left, her husband went with them. 'At first he send me money, sometimes 200,000 P at a time, but now I don't hear from him much. But I have the baby and he doesn't.' As she spoke, she sighed more and more frequently. 'Before, Qui Nhon number one. Beaucoup money. Now *ti-ti* (little) Americans and I very poor. I number ten in my heart'. Thinking about those good old days made her feel warm to me, who must have appeared in her café like a surrogate American, and it was just nostalgia that prompted her farewell words: 'You come back to Qui Nhon and we sleep together. Okay?' I liked her, but not quite enough to go back to Qui Nhon.

Danang

If there was one place I hated more than Qui Nhon it was Danang, the second city of South Vietnam and a major port. It recalled to me the words of a nineteenth-century British sailor who described Freetown, Sierra Leone, as 'the Devil's *poste restante*'. It was here that the Marines landed in 1965, the first US unit to take part in the war, and it was here that the Marines held sway until their collapse in 1968. The Marines were also in charge of the Press Centre, where all we journalists were obliged to stay or lose our privileges of transport and cheap Scotch.

In the previous book I described some of the 'civic action' programmes undertaken by the Marines in the lowlands near Danang. They were proud of these efforts to 'win the hearts and minds' of the people but still more proud of their aggressive campaigns in the mountains further west. In this slender waist of Vietnam the Americans held the coastal strip, with most of the population, but the Communists occupied most of the mountainous jungle stretching towards Laos and North Vietnam. This misty wilderness, broken by hills and ravines, was used by the Communists as a training ground and supply base. Each spring and sometimes at other times of the year the Americans made an attack to dislodge the Communists from their fastness in the west. These attacks, called by fatuous names like Operation Hastings, Operation Masher or Operation Gamekeeper, were launched from Danang which was therefore the city one visited to learn about the war. It was assumed by the Marines at the Press Centre that every journalist wished to attend these military operations, so that, willy nilly, one sometimes had to go. Once I asked if I could get a ride on a helicopter to Hue. 'Sure, sure,' said the sergeant, and drove me out to the airport, where I met a sad-looking group of newspaper men and was put with them on a helicopter that went to a desolate place called Camp Eagle. Becoming suspicious, I asked once more if there would be a helicopter taking me to Hue and the same sergeant repeated: 'Sure, sure.' Ten minutes later I was aboard a much bigger helicopter, which set off in a westward direction as a half-witted officer announced that he could promise us a 'real good fire-fight' and added that eight American helicopters had been shot down that day round the place to which we were going. We arrived in the rain at a red earth clearing, raw as a wound in the jungle, which here consisted of dead and broken trees. Heavy guns were firing in all directions into the forest and it occurred to me that although these Americans probably did not know where the Communists were, the Communists probably knew where we were. And so they did, for within a few minutes mortars or rockets crashed into our camp which I think was called Bastogne, after a battle in France. An American TV journalist (who was later killed in Cambodia) was not satisfied with the quantity of the attack and demanded to go to the next camp, Khe San I think, where the 'fire fight' would be more spectacular. 'But this kind of war is meaningless,' I said to him, and he agreed but went on: 'My company just wants film with the most bangs and the most dead bodies, and I like to show those people at home how bloody and pointless this war is'. While this TV man was asking to travel west I was asking to go back east to Hue, Camp Eagle or even Danang, which was where I was taken, of course. That evening the colonel in charge of the Press Centre found to his disgust that five of the reporters present were Europeans, a people whom he distrusted. 'If I were President of the United States', he informed the *Le Monde* correspondent, 'the first thing I'd do would be to drop a hydrogen bomb on Paris.' He was not joking.

On my next visit to Danang, a few weeks later, I determined to stay away from the Press Centre and take a room at the Grand Hotel. I also decided to stay away from the war and to do something enjoyable, namely visit the West German hospital ship that was then moored off the front. When this ship had first come to Vietnam and was moored in Saigon, some German newspaper carried a scandalous, lip-smacking article on the activities of the nurses, one of whom, so it was said, had allowed herself to be stripped, tied to an anchor and taken by all comers. Full of hope, I boarded the ship at Danang presented a visiting card and was introduced to a big, disapproving matron like an ageing Brunnhilde who had just been cheeked by one of the junior Valkyries. She gave me a tour which was thankfully quick—until we arrived at the napalm ward. As I forced myself to glance at, if not examine these roasted, pain-racked bodies, mostly of women and children, the matron explained to me: 'Almost none of the victims live more than three weeks even if they survive the burns. They die of poisoning of the kidneys.' I was so shocked by the napalm ward that I did not think to protest when the matron said afterwards: 'I will now arrange for you to see the Vietnamese state hospital in Danang,' but it turned out to be less alarming. Like other state hospitals I had seen in this country, its lack of equipment and sanitation were in part balanced out by the friendly atmosphere, in which relatives of the patients could wander and even camp in the wards. Furthermore there were only a few napalm cases, since most of these went to the hospital ship or, as I suspect, were eased out of their agony. On this same trip to Danang I met two American military doctors who told me categorically that there were no civilian victims of napalm. They just would not believe what I had seen and been told at the hospital ship. They were humane, liberal people and I suspect that, knowing the horror of napalm, they could not live with the thought that their country was using this weapon, even in error, to kill women and children. At about this time a group of American doctors toured Vietnam and reported that all burns attributed to napalm were due to the use of 'unfamiliar cooking fluid'. Apparently they had not been told by their interpreters that the Vietnamese word for napalm is gasoline.

It was at Danang in the American time that one saw most painfully the sheer profusion and waste of industrial military matter. Great alps of ammunition were stacked on the dock-side next to an Andes chain of crates and containers of Pepsi Cola, plastic boots, transistor radios, baseball bats, electricity generators, air-conditioners, candy and pulp magazines. Every company in the United States would seem to have dumped here its goods, soon to become garbage. To this physical super-abundance was added the noise and the petrol stench of innumerable trucks, tanks, tankers, jeeps and personnel carriers, all causing mud in the wet season and dust in the dry.

At the time one imagined that all this material and noise were necessary to the war effort. Yet five years later, when fighting was still in progress and more than a million men still served in ARVIN, practically no goods were arriving at Danang. The sea front was uncluttered; instead of newly un-loaded tanks and artillery one saw a tiny open museum of rusting and broken tanks and artillery, captured last year from the Communists. Of course much of the material for the ARVIN troops in this region now comes from Saigon on the road which was once impassable, yet still I wonder if all those American goods really helped the war, if they were not rather dumped at Danang, in the literal and economic sense, by American capitalism.

The American presence was nowhere more evident than in Danang; and in no place these days is one more struck by the American absence. Indeed sometimes an American seeing another white man will greet him and ask him what he is doing in town. Gone is that class of Vietnamese who lived off Americans. Gone are the black market stalls, from one of which I had too hurriedly purchased a US military uniform, only to find when I was wearing it in the field that the patches of what I had thought was dirt was the dried (now melting) blood of the deceased previous owner. The Cocktail Bar has been closed down, as have the next door offices of the 'Organ of Forces Fighting for Freedom in Vietnam'—whatever on earth that was. At one roadside stall dealing mostly in plastic Buddhas I found a touching reminder of the former American presence. These were some of those three-sided plaques made of marble or dark wood, which people inscribe with their name and display on their office desk by way of introduction to visitors: 'Albert C. Tucker, USAF', or 'Mr Piter Starr'. But some of these plaques had clearly been made as mementos, 'Dave Hook. Vietnam 1970–71' 'Danang, Rocket City. 1969–70', or 'Rock and Jessie. Always', surrounding a pierced heart.

The people who had commissioned these objects must either have died, have forgotten them, or sold them back to the stall-holders who now purvey them as archaeological artefacts of a vanished civilisation.

This last fancy occurred to me because I had noticed the ornaments just after visiting the Danang Museum of artefacts from the age of the Chams, the race conquered and almost killed off by the Vietnamese about six hundred years ago. To judge by their statues and miniature temples, the Chams were akin by culture and race to the Khmers, who built Angkor Wat in Cambodia. As I learned on my visit, the Vietnamese feel guilty about the way they treated the Chams—only 30,000 of whom now survive—believing that they will suffer for this for generations to come.* The Danang Museum had been shut during the 1960's but I had a look around thanks to the US Marines who were guarding it as part of the 'civil action' programme. Since then, I see with sorrow, there are several more statues without heads, a fact which the custodian attributed to rocket attacks but which, I suspect, may also have been done by souvenir-seekers. However no harm has come to the Goddess Tara from Duong Binh, a thick-lipped, ugly, imperious woman with big breasts and a full belly bulging under her tight-waisted sarong. Nor has harm come to the Buddha from Dong Duong, in Quang Ngai, whose stern and autocratic face contrasts with the gentler Buddhas of Angkor Wat. He is shown seated with legs wide apart and hands on knees, and round the base of the statue there is a bas-relief frieze showing Amforas, or dancing girls. But whereas at Angkor Wat these girls would be shown full face and smiling, here they are leaning on one arm with down-cast stare, like a

* The Chams who survive in South Vietnam maintain their religion and have refused to inter-marry with Vietnamese. In November 1973 I went to a Cham village near Phan Rang, at which I was hospitably received, but the militiamen threatened to shoot the Vietnamese taxi-driver simply because he was Vietnamese.

melancholy *vahine* in a Gauguin painting. All these works date from the 5th and 6th century A.D.

There is much to be said for a city that re-opens such a museum in time of war and in range of enemy shelling. Indeed Danang, although still not a pleasant place, is so much pleasanter than before as to be almost unrecognizable. The rubbish gets collected, the pavements have been repaired and blue paint applied to government buildings. The shops have been cleaned up, there are elegant new cafés and two good floating restaurants in the harbour. Some of the credit for this cleaning up goes to experts provided by Shell, the Dutch-British company, who run the oil storage tanks in Danang and sell a lot of its petrol. The French, too, have moved back in force to fill a bit of the vacuum left by the Americans. They now provide many schoolteachers, while their Cultural Centre rivals the buildings of Shell, the US Consul and the Governor of the province. But mostly it is the Vietnamese who have replaced the Americans. Even the insults to European journalists are now handed out by Vietnamese, not American colonels. In a restaurant one lunch-time I noticed I was being stared by a colonel in the Rangers, a regiment notorious for its use of torture and murder. At last he came over and said: 'I remember you,' which he probably did, for I could remember him—without fondness. 'Aren't you the journalist that speaks fluent Chinese?' he began, wrong first time. 'No, I'm sorry,' I said, 'I can't remember you.' 'What's your name?' 'West'. 'Surely you have a first name?' I showed him my press card, which he studied with care and some signs of disapproval. Before going back to his table (and an annoyingly pretty woman) he sneered and said: 'You journalists make good money in this country'. I kept silent and thought of those cheques from *The Listener*.

In Danang, just as everywhere in Vietnam these days, there is distress about the economic problem. A Chinese in the Vietnamese army complained that Danang got none of the industry of the south. What hope was there for the future, I asked a Vietnamese who had invested his war-time profits as a tailor at Dong Ha in a lavish, even trendy restaurant, the Salon Danube, complete with impressionist paintings, suits of armour, bits of contorted tree branches and French food. He was utterly confident in his future: 'This year, it's true, there are not so many Americans, but soon they will be back—drilling for oil. At the moment most of the oil men are in Saigon, but there's lots of oil up here, round Hue, and the drilling will have to be done from Danang as it's the safest base.'

It must be the curse of the Chams that has doomed Danang to be first a war town and then an oil town: from Armageddon to Abu Dhabi, from Hell to Shell.

Hue 1968

Until Tet 1968, the northernmost city of Hue was the one place in South Vietnam where almost nothing happened. It is true that in 1966 the Buddhists rioted, threw stones at the troops and burned the US Information Centre, but soon afterwards Hue returned to its usual torpor. (The gutted Centre was not rebuilt and now serves a much more useful purpose by sheltering squatter families). Hue seldom appeared in the news and, when it did, was almost invariably called the ancient, imperial capital,* as though its history counted for more than its present. Because of this lack of interest on the part of the outside world, Hue guarded the character of the old Vietnam, almost untouched by the idiocies of the war. There were few Americans, little motor traffic and no mortar attacks at night. The Citadel and the nearby tombs were claimed as tourist attractions, although none of these buildings dates back further than 1800 and some were designed in the Twenties, Odeon style. The city's greatest attraction has always been the Perfume River,

* A mistranslation of the French *ancienne capitale impériale*, or 'former imperial capital'.

sluggish but busy with sampans, fishing boats and even sculling vessels, for this university city, sometimes compared to Oxford, has long been famous for boat races. It is also an aristocratic, some would say snobbish city, that has produced many Vietnamese leaders, including the Emperor Bao Dai, his successor Ngo Dinh Diem and their arch-foe, Vo Nguyen Giap, the North Vietnamese general. The children of the bourgeoisie attend the famous Hue Lycée and it is always a pleasure to watch the girl students cycling home over the river, the tails of their white *ao dai* uniforms tucked under the carriers. Oddly anough, almost every Vietnamese I have met outside Vietnam was an old boy or girl of this lycée. Like Scotland, the narrow waist of Vietnam has always been poor in money but rich in talent, driving the children away in emigration. Like Scotland, especially the Highlands, Hue is obsessed with a feeling of melancholy, of regret for the past and of anxiety for the future. This melancholy has been deepened by the events of the last six years.

The battle for Hue, that opened at Tet 1968, has been well described by journalists who were present. Much has been written, too, but with rather more passion than scholarship, of the mass graves unearthed in the months that followed the fighting. It was claimed by the Americans (and repeated eagerly by their British friends like Bernard Levin and Kingsley Amis) that all the occupants of these graves had been murdered by the Communists when they first took the city. However some of the graves were not discovered, or not made public, till long after Hue was retaken and 'pacified' by government troops and police under the leadership of General Loan, well known to the world for the photograph of him shooting a Communist prisoner. In the months following Tet the ruthless-ness of the war increased with frightening intensity, as was disclosed at the inquiry into the My Lai massacre. People I know in Hue are much less certain than Levin and Amis that those in the mass graves were all victims of communism.

In 1968 I did not get to Hue until more than a month after the end of the fighting. Having failed to get there by helicopter and not wanting to risk the journey by road from Danang, I succeeded in getting a lift on a small ship of the US Navy. It was a squat, flat-bottomed, ugly vessel that did not inspire confidence. Nor did its crew. Except for the worried Negro captain, myself and Murray Sayle of the *Sunday Times*, there was not a sober man on board when we left Danang in the early evening. Indeed some of the crew had arrived so drunk that they could scarcely board at all. They had brought liquor with them and they went below as we set sail, leaving the deck, the bridge and the view of the lights of Danang to Murray, myself and the anxious skipper, who was grasping the wheel with both hands throughout the voyage.

Soon after dawn we reached the mouth of the Perfume River, about ten miles downstream from the city itself. It must have been some Buddhist holiday, for the fishing boats carried streamers of red or green instead of the yellow-and-orange marzipan flag of the Republic of Vietnam. 'The fishermen are not hostile,' I was told by one of the crew who had come up on deck for air to ease his hangover. Shortly afterwards he and another sailor went to the lengths of manning one of the heavy machine-guns with which the vessel was armed. The first sailor took aim at a group of old women plodding along the bank and muttered a 'rata-tat-tat' from between his teeth. 'What are you playing at?' asked his friend, to which the first sailor replied: 'Playing war games, I suppose.' Further upstream, we started to pass wrecked and burned-out houses and pagodas, and over the paddy fields we could see the Phantom jets strafing the equally phantom Communists.'Up here the people are VC,' the first sailor said, and went down to join the rest of the crew in the kitchen, or galley, the safest part of the ship, leaving the deck, the wheel and the guns once more to Murray, myself and the Negro captain.

I had lunch that day with some Vietnamese acquaintances

who ran a tailor's shop near the market. They had not been harmed by the Communists but part of their roof had been holed by a shell of one side or the other. Kind and hospitable, in spite of their own troubles, they urged me to sleep at their house as they said (fallaciously) that my third-storey hotel room was vulnerable to mortars. I turned down the invitation because, though I did not say so, I preferred a sprung mattress to one of the wooden tables that served their house for beds.

From press reports at the time I had expected to find Hue flattened like Hamburg or Dresden after the Second World War, but there was not much sign of damage. The one-storey, wooden houses north of the river are almost as easy to rebuild as to knock down, while the former French part of the city, south of the river, had not been much hit by heavy artillery fire. Most of the bombardment, including naval artillery used against individual snipers, had been directed on the Citadel itself. This showed so little sign of damage afterwards that some Americans claimed to have spared a historic monument, just as the Royal Air Force claimed to have spared Cologne Cathedral during the Second World War. The fact is that the walls of Hue Citadel had been built so strong that the shells scarcely dented them, just as the British bombs bounced off Cologne Cathedral.

The Cercle Sportif, which the French built by the river in 1939, survived in spirit if not altogether in substance. There were several shell holes in the walls and some cad had looted the billiard balls; but the food had improved, there was still plenty of beer and the membership had stayed steady. All this was in large part due to the good Jacques Sanlaville, a big, red-faced and hearty Burgundian, who has spent more than twenty years in this country, first with the French Army and then at Hue power station. I found him at his accustomed seat in the Cercle Sportif, holding a big glass of beer, but I noticed that some of his fingers were missing. This was not the result of the fighting at Tet but of an ambush the year before in which he received several bullets. 'I managed to drive back to Hue,' he explained. 'My Vietnamese assistant, sitting next to me wasn't touched but he spent two months in hospital suffering from shock'.

The Sanlaville home by the power station had been overrun by the Communists on the first day of Tet but no harm came to Sanlaville, his Cambodian wife or their many engaging children. I heard later from other sources that Sanlaville showed great courage and had some success in persuading the Communists to release certain captured Europeans. One of these, a French girl reporter, later published a rather wild version of what had happened—to Sanlaville's lasting fury. The Communists stayed on in Sanlaville's house, which was shelled by the Americans with anti-personnel *flechettes*—barbed, inch-long arrows of steel that explode in all directions from a canister with deadly force. Two months later Sanlaville showed me his trees, which were so profusely embedded with flechettes that I gave up trying to count them. When the Communists were pushed out the US Marines moved in, smashing everything that could be smashed in the Sanlaville home, down to the children's dolls. They even cut out the seats of the chairs to make them into lavatories.

The massacres were discussed with remarkable lack of excitement. 'It was rather like France after the liberation,' said one Frenchman. 'The Communists had a list of people they thought were traitors, but others got killed for purely personal reasons. They were denounced by servants or by people with grudges.' A planter from Khe Sanh, who had come to Hue that fatal Tet 'to get a holiday from the war,' was staying with priests when the Communists came. 'They shot two priests dead. I was shot in the leg but they left it at that. They didn't kill me. Another priest was not harmed. He had a box with about 16,000 piastres which were the church funds. He tried to hide the box under his robes but the Communists told him to produce it. They took it and gave him a receipt. A few days later he was noticed by two of his former students who were serving with the Viet Cong. They told their commander: "This man is a friend of the Vietnamese. He was always good to his students." So then the priest produced his receipt and the Viet Cong gave him his money back.' Most of the people killed by the Communists were policemen, politicians and civil servants, but some priests, teachers and doctors were shot as well. Such things do happen in long civil wars.

One day I was walking with Murray Sayle over Clemenceau bridge, which had been partly blown up and was closed to motorised traffic. We passed four Communist suspects, three boys and a girl, who were being led, blindfolded and handcuffed by an American and a Vietnamese soldier. The American told me that these suspects, who were aged about eighteen, had spent a few days at a police station and now were going to the ARVIN for more interrogation. When I asked if they would afterwards go to prison the soldier looked at me with surprise before answering 'Maybe'. Murray and I followed the party into an ARVIN compound where we met a second American, a corporal in intelligence. The first American said: 'I've brought you some more meat,' and the second one answered: 'Yeah, and I see some of it's female.' We saw the prisoners taken into a shed where a tough ARVIN man singled out one of the boys, gave him a violent boot in the testicles, punched his head, then kicked him again in the base of the stomach. This interrogation process seemed to be quite routine, and at first Murray and I were too surprised to protest. When we did protest, the intelligence corporal, who was a southerner, said with all the courtesy of his people: 'I'd appreciate it if you gentlemen were to leave the compound.'

Later that day I fell into chat with a young US infantryman, who held strong views about Hue: 'You know that bridge that was blown up? They should clear it away and build a four-lane flyover. This could be a real nice city. It's a pity the people aren't civilised.'

Hue 1971

When I next came to Hue, late in 1971, the wrecked bridge had been repaired by the same Eiffel company that had built the original and had also repaired it in 1945, when it was first blown up. The same French company had meanwhile constructed a second bridge, in a shallow and graceful arch, a few hundred yards upstream. The contracts given to Eiffel struck some Americans as a deliberate snub to the country that saved Hue in Tet 1968; but one should not expect gratitude from one's allies. On this occasion I noticed two wall slogans, apparently by the same hand: 'Americans go home!' and 'Smash down the American attempt of Vietnamisation of the war!' Did the slogan writer demand that Americans go home yet continue fighting? Certainly Vietnamisation of the war had not proved very effective. The Communists had moved nearer the coast and a counter-attack in Laos had ended in failure early in 1972. This battle was memorable for the photograph that turned stomachs all over the world—of an Arvin soldier attempting to flee by hanging to the skids of a helicopter.

Most Hue people I met feared that a new offensive was coming (it came four months later, in April 1972) and were not very confident in the outcome. Winter, which is both damp and cold in Hue, added an extra degree of melancholy to the Cercle Sportif. Drizzle and mist hung over the Perfume River, while indoors there sounded plaintive Vietnamese music from cracked and furry gramophone records. It was a Chekhov scene with Chekhov characters supplied by the Cercle Sportif. 'You're frightened of lung cancer?' a doctor asked, when I declined a cigarette. 'Well I can tell you in all my years of practice here, I've never seen one case of lung cancer. Cancer of the uterus and of the breast, yes, but here in Vietnam there are too many other things from which to die. We smoke because we're unhappy, because of the war and because we're poor'. The doctor's legs began to shake, as often happens to

Vietnamese when they start to talk politics. 'Are you going to see the Communists?' When I said I would like to, but it was hard to arrange, he lowered his voice and said that the real enemy were not the Communists but the Americans.

A navy colonel, whose brothers and sisters are all in Europe, spoke lovingly of his fishing-rods and the big bream up-river. He offered to take me fishing but could not stick to his offer because upstream was not safe, while in Hue all the fish had been killed off by hand-grenades. On several occasions the Cercle Sportif rocked from the blast of grenades thrown into the water. A literary man regretted the time when you could take a walk to the source of the Perfume River: 'There were iguanas, sometimes elephants and always fish, like trout, as many as you could catch. It was a place for lovers and poets, but it's fifteen years now since it was safe to go there or to the Hill of Clouds on the way to Danang.' His friend pointed over the river towards the Citadel. 'Do you remember, only five years ago, how it used to be all red with flamboyants? Now they've cut down most of the trees and those that remain don't produce any flowers.' A civil servant complained that all our ideas have been turned upside down: 'A cyclo-driver makes more now than an engineer. We say that the Perfume River flows upstream'. A helicopter pilot, who had been flying a mission that day, spoke only about Cambodia, where he had been in time of peace: 'Before the fall of Sihanouk it was the last paradise, the last paradise.' Even Sanlaville, seldom a victim of melancholy, grew wistful about his native Burgundy: 'There's marvellous cheese, great slices of fresh bread and as much red wine as you can drink.'

The older people in Hue speak French but most of those in their twenties and thirties have learned some kind of English. A naval lieutenant, whose legs shook incessantly as he spoke, listened twice a day to BBC broadcasts and was interested in Britain and her problems. 'Could you tell me, Sir, why your leader Heath is not "married." Is he a swinger like Premier

Trudeau of Canada? Wouldn't you agree, Sir, that Southern Rhodesia has the only civilised government in Africa? It will take many years to civilise the Negroes, won't it, Sir?' A still more earnest young man gave me a card introducing himself as Hue Chapter Treasurer of the Vietnam Junior Chamber of Commerce. In turn I gave him a yellowing card of the *New Statesman*, for which I had written for some years, on and off. He glanced at it and then looked up with an expression of eagerness and delight that I could not connect with that journal. 'Are you a Christian, Sir?' Before I could mumble the usual evasive reply, he burst out: 'I'm a Gideon, Sir. That is the Gideon sign on my tie. You will have seen our Gideon Bibles in all the best hotels of Saigon—in the Caravelle, the Majestic and the Continental. Unfortunately, Sir, our hotels here in Hue aren't yet good enough, but I can assure you, Sir, that when you come back to Hue in a year, you'll find a Gideon Bible in your hotel room.' He must have sensed that this news did not enthral me, for he took another look at the visiting card. 'Richard West, New Statesman', he read out loud, then added sadly: 'I'm sorry, Sir, when I looked at the card first time I thought it said "Richard West, New Testament".'

Hue 1973

It was nearly two years before I returned to Hue but sure enough there were Gideon Bibles displayed in the new hotel, or so I am told, for I did not visit the bedrooms. The hotel is called 'Victory', written in English, which may be an earnest of faith or a sly joke, like the title of Conrad's novel.

The Communist offensive beginning in April 1972 took Dong Ha, Quang Tri and most of the province of which Hue is the capital. Thousands of refugees abandoned Hue itself, including the major part of the administration. 'It was like France in 1940,' said Sanlaville, who managed to get his own family to Danang. However he himself stayed in Hue and kept going the two organisations he loves—the Cercle Sportif and the power station. Most of the journalists in Hue at the time appeared to believe that its fall was approaching, but the Communists could not take the town, or perhaps did not intend to—it is always rash to guess at their military objectives. The South Vietnamese units that had abandoned Quang Tri were replaced by the skilled and courageous Marines, who at last retook that city.

After a few months the offensive came to a halt and the negotiations began which led to the so-called ceasefire of February 1973. The Communists had established control over a lot of territory but few people, and nowhere were they more ominous than in the northernmost region near Hue. Moreover the Communist military strength in the south has reached great proportions. According to Saigon government sources late in 1973, the Communists at that time had up to 600,000 troops, many hundreds of tanks and twelve military airports in South Vietnam, one of which, Khe San, can take jet fighter aircraft. The build-up of Communist weapon power is astonishing and alarming, when one considers their former feeble equipment. In 1966 I had gone by road from Dong Ha to a mountainous area, known I believe as the 'rockpile', where American planes were bombing and dropping napalm on Communists in the middle distance. To relieve the boredom an officer showed me and a colleague the equipment captured during the last few days. Besides the usual rice, toothpaste and medical kits there were some of the poorest weapons I have seen—ancient rifles, too big for the Vietnamese, home-made bazookas and mortars mounted on iron wheels. I remarked to my colleague that if the Communists were prepared to fight with that sort of primitive equipment they would be deadly if armed with artillery or even planes. This condition had been fulfilled by 1973. Dong Ha airport was held by the Communists while a Red Chinese ship was in Dong Ha port. Communist heavy artillery and at least one armoured division had entrenched themselves within range of Hue and presumably were prepared to attack if the ceasefire was formally ended. On this latest trip to Hue an ARVIN officer told me casually that he had spent the day watching the North Vietnamese move up their troops by lorry. 'If they attack a third time', he told me, 'just pack your bags.'

The ever-increasing military menace has added to the melancholy of Hue. One morning a student who wanted to practise his English came up and said: 'Are you American? Because you are standing on the river bank, you must be thinking about poetry.' As a matter of fact I was thinking if it was time for my first beer of the day, but I heard out the young man's stilted, practised phrases. 'I am studying at the English faculty. Last year my brother who was in the army was killed near here and since then I am lazy, I cannot work because I do not want to live. Do you believe in the Regeneration of Vietnam?' (This was the title of a government propaganda campaign.) 'At the university very few people believe in it. They do not believe in any future but war and therefore they want to ruin their body and their spirit. Do you like warfare? I do not, but there are many people here who have grown rich because of the war.' These were typical of the remarks that you generally hear from students. What touched me was the dimension of time. I had heard the same views, in almost the same words, expressed by students of the same age in Hue in 1966. During the Fifties an earlier generation must have regarded the future with similar hopelessness. For the young men there has always been the prospect of military service, to which has been added in recent years the prospect of war in their home town.

Of course there are some imperturbables. On this visit I stayed as guest of the ebullient Jacques Sanlaville, whose kindness over the years has been great. He has acquired a movie projector to show films sent up by the Alliance Française as well as a tape recorder to play his favourite German brass-band music and martial songs from around the world. This particular tape, which includes the 'Chasseurs Alpins' and

'Scotland the Brave' is marred for Sanlaville by 'The Halls of Montezuma' the song of the US Marine Corps who ravaged his home. And many Vietnamese still come to Hue for the peace that prevails as long as the war does not intrude. At the Sportif this time I met Trinh Con Son, Vietnam's most famous writer of songs, who told me that he had come to Hue for '*du calme*'.

One ARVIN officer who had served seven years told me: 'I'm going abroad. I've done my duty. I can't go through it again.' But it is always dangerous to exaggerate defeatism in South Vietnam. The Americans did so, jeering at ARVIN troops and contributing to their depression; but the Americans have departed and ARVIN fights on. It is argued that the Communists must prevail because they have fought so long and made such sacrifices, but the anti-Communist Vietnamese have fought just as long and made comparable sacrifices—fifty Vietnamese officers in the French Army volunteered to be dropped into Dien Bien Phu on the day before it was captured. True, only a handful of South Vietnamese have such ideological certainty as the Communists, but they are kept going by stoicism, romantic and very Vietnamese, that reconciles them to death.

A comparison has been made with the fall of France, but even in France, where defeatism was widespread, there were hundreds of thousands prepared to fight against all odds. In Hue on this last visit I chanced to be reading *Pilote de Guerre* by Antoine de Saint-Exupery, the poet and pilot who served in the French air force until his death in 1942. During the German invasion of France he was pilot of a reconnaissance plane flying perilous and probably useless missions behind the enemy lines. One passage seemed most appropriate to the mood in Hue:

> Is my mind filled with the thought of the war of the Nazi against the Occident? Not at all. I think in terms of immediate details. I think of possible wounds. I think of the absurdity of

flying over German-held Arras at two thousand feet; of the futility of the Intelligence we are asked to bring back; of the interminable time it takes to dress in these clothes that remind me of men made ready for the executioner. And I think of my gloves. Where the devil are my gloves? I have lost my gloves.

I can no longer see the cathedral in which I live. I am dressing for the service of a dead god.

Part Three
HIGHLANDS

The outside world thinks of South Vietnam as a small country of jungle or paddy fields, crowded with peasants in black pyjamas and conical hats. In fact most of its territory consists of rolling hills and savanna land, whose scant population is not Vietnamese either in language or race. There is much argument over the origin of these highlanders, whom the Vietnamese call *moi* (savage), the French call Montagnards and the Americans call tribespeople. One legend says that at the beginning of time a dog, a buffalo and a woman were arguing which should drink first at a river, when the dog killed and ate the buffalo, then mated the woman to start the Montagnard race. Another legend, of greater political acumen, says that when all the world's peoples crawled out of holes in the ground, the Montagnards were not fast enough and lost their share of good land. Anthropologists now suggest that some of the Montagnards descend from the Chams, who were chased from the coast by the Vietnamese about 600 years ago, while the rest descend from Polynesians who sailed here about three thousand years ago.

Until colonial times the Montagnards lived, undisturbed and ignored, in the hinterland of both North and South Vietnam and in parts of Cambodia and Laos. Although differing widely in language, most of these tribes shared a way of life based on hunting, 'slash and burn' farming and matriarchy. They usually lived in thatched, wooden 'long-houses' raised on stilts; they wore the sarong, enjoyed gong music and rice wine and went in fear of evil spirits who could be stopped from mischief only by animal sacrifice, especially of the buffalo, which had to be tied to a post and beaten to death. Since the Montagnards were pacific and docile, the French largely ignored them except to exact a small annual village tax and two weeks' work on the roads. Both the French and the first leaders of independent South Vietnam banned the Vietnamese from all but those parts of the highlands where they were needed as servants and artisans.

This isolation was breached in the late Fifties, when both sides in the Vietnamese civil war sought to establish themselves in the territory of the Montagnards. The Communists wanted bases, supply routes and training grounds for their attack on the coastal strip; the Saigon government wanted to counter the Communists and to provide land for refugees, especially the Catholics who had left North Vietnam. The Montagnards, indifferent to all ideologies, were wooed, threatened and terrorised by both sides who needed their help as porters, auxiliary troops and providers of food.

The Americans, in their time, presented themselves to the Montagnards as friends and protectors against the Vietnamese of Saigon as well as Hanoi. This approach, based often on genuine sympathy, was returned by some of the Montagnards who served as irregular troops and joined the Protestant churches run by American missionaries. Yet even before 1968 and the start of the American debacle, it was obvious that the Montagnards could not forever rely on the help and protection of the Americans. The US advisers in the highlands, although preferring the Montagnards to the Vietnamese, knew that they could not flout the authority of the government for the sake of a weak minority. And even before 1968 people of Vietnamese race were moving into the highlands, first as officials and soldiers, then as traders, farmers and plantation owners. A large part of the million or so Montagnards have been removed from their ancestral lands, forced into camps and deprived of their feasts, their gongs and their religious rites.

The highlands were never much publicised at the height of the Vietnam war; they seemed a confusing side-issue, remote from the fighting and politics of the belligerent Vietnamese. Sometimes *Newsweek* or one of the other liberal newspapers would bring the plight of the Montagnards to the attention of its readers, but it seemed a small cause for concern among so many greater horrors. Americans in the highlands often compared the fate of the Montagnards to that of the Indians in the American West, whose destruction had been so painfully chronicled in *Bury My Heart at Wounded Knee*. But feeling ashamed of the greed and cruelty of their ancestors, the Americans feel unable to criticise when the same crimes are committed by modern Vietnamese. They have therefore looked on with sadness and resignation. The sadness is still more poignant because it was here in the highlands, and only here, that the Americans once felt appreciated and liked for what they did in Vietnam.

Dalat

The resort town of Dalat, high in the mountains north-east of Saigon, is always described as a place untouched by the war and always enjoys the briefest of curfews. In fact there are many Communist troops in the surrounding province and most of Dalat was seized at Tet 1968. When I was there in May the same year, Communist troops in civilian clothes once more entered the town, which sprawls over so large an area that one suburb does not know what is happening in the others. I was already the only guest in the large, silent Palace Hotel, whose receptionists in their brown sweaters were knitting intently and said to me '*Beaucoup peur*', over and over again, like the plaintive cry of a marsh bird. On the last day the receptionists, the chef and still worse the barman, failed to turn up for work and I was left with the porter alone in this now rather alarming hotel. Next morning I went for a walk to try and find out what was happening, until I was stopped by a kindly man who said: 'Get away from here, they're all VC.' I took his advice and went to Saigon.

My next visit, five and a half years later, was made during the tourist season, which largely explained the jollier atmosphere. The hotel looked the same, down to the knitting receptionists, the stuffed stoats and the tough carrots; however the duck press and the tame deer appear to have vanished, while marijuana was smoked after dinner instead of cigars. I have often noticed that when Vietnamese go on holiday they look as though they are having a good time, all the time; and so it was in Dalat. Couples walked hand in hand through the dripping pine forests or drove their pedalos across the artificial lake. For the first time since the early Sixties dancing has been permitted in clubs and bars (until quite recently it was forbidden even at private parties, which used to be raided after tip-offs to the police) but I noticed that all the girls knew the steps of dances almost forgotten now in England, such as the rumba, the fox trot and the tango.

The air is delicious after the gasoline fumes of Saigon. Indeed Dalat is a most pleasant if slightly boring town, which helps to account for its reputation of peacefulness. If you stroll out in the evening to be met by bursts of machine-gun fire sending tracers overhead, it is easy to think, as one normally thinks in Vietnam, that this is merely the ARVIN giving a signal or having a celebration. Just before leaving Dalat a few days later, I started to chat with a Frenchman who asked me what I was doing there. When I answered 'Journalist', he said: 'I see. You've come up because of the fighting.' He could not believe that I did not know of the fighting or of the rockets that had fallen in town a few days before. I mention this to show the atmosphere of vague and confused anxiety that prevails even in towns like Dalat since the vague and confused cease-fire.

Most of the Montagnards near Dalat belong to the people known by their language as the Koho's (the vowel sounds are pronounced and stressed as in the English 'guffaw') who number over 100,000. In colonial days they were left alone by the French who considered them too idle for servants, too stupid to learn French and too superstitious to grasp either the Catholic faith or the Republican Rights of Man. The Koho's, for their part, were content to stay in their fastnesses, drinking rice wine and communing muzzily with their favourite spirits of frog, mountain and morning dew. The Koho's were first roused from ancestral lethargy by the efforts of Herbert A. Jackson, an American who came to Dalat in the Thirties for the Christian and Missionary Alliance. Although the French would not allow him at first into the Montagnard villages, he and Mrs Jackson established a 'tribes center' in Dalat itself, at which promising Montagnards were invited to study. Two of these tribesmen, Sau and his brother Kar, are the heroes of a devout book, *The Bamboo Cross. The Witness of Christian Martyrs in the Communist-ridden Jungles of Viet Nam*, by Homer H. Dowdy (author of *Christ's Witchdoctors*). I read this book with a sense of nostalgia. When I was doing research on West African history, I became quite a connoisseur of missionary works of the Dowdy genre. If one substitutes slave-trader for communist, Yoruba for Koho, fetish-worship for spirit-worship, and trade gin for rice wine, *The Bamboo Cross* is a missionary tale of West Africa in the nineteenth century. We learn how the boy Sau first visits Dalat and glimpses the marvels of modern science—'he (Jackson) was talking to the end of a black stick held to his mouth and ear'—how he came to love Jesus and went back to his village to pray for the heathen souls—'old mother, I wish to talk about you to the Spirit of the Skies.' We read of the Montagnards' stubborn addiction to alcohol, their backsliding, the chains that still link them to Satan. 'They live in daily terror of evil spirits,' said Jackson, who wished them to live in terror of hell-fire everlasting.

The second section of Dowdy's book, which was read with

awe by pious American servicemen, concerns the struggle between the Viet Cong and the recently Christianised Montagnards. As early as 1956 the Province Chief at Dalat decreed that the Montagnards in this region must move out of the mountains to resettle in villages in the plains, where they would be less open to pressure from the Communists. Many tribespeople were unwilling to leave their ancestral burial grounds, their upland methods of farming and their bad but familiar spirits, whom they at least knew how to appease. The Communists in the mountains played on these fears, for they needed the Montagnards as recruits and suppliers of food, but Sau and the church leaders spoke for resettlement and helped establish lowland villages near Nhatrang. *The Bamboo Cross* reaches its not very hair-raising climax when 'cold, glowering' Communists enter this resettled village to try to persuade the Montagnards to renounce their faith and to go back into the mountains. Two Christian leaders protest and are kidnapped and killed; the rest flee down-river to safety, protected by God. This escape would sound still more miraculous if it were not clear from Dowdy's account that the Communists on the bank neither fired on the rafts nor made serious efforts to stop them.

At Tet 1968 the Communists did make martyrs of Christian Montagnards in the province. At one village I visited, Maté, three men had been shot in front of the church door, although it is not known if they were chosen because of their faith or because they were pro-government village chiefs. In the attack on Dalat the Communists entered the grounds of the Alliance Mission but did not find, or apparently try to find the missionaries who were concealed there. 'The Lord's hand hid us from harm', I was told by Helen Evans, a niece of the Jacksons and one of the doughtiest missionaries in the country.

In spite of Communist menaces and the bad security of the region, the Alliance HQ in the United States has poured money and effort into the highlands of Vietnam. (In my last book I quoted one of their leaflets: 'WAR? YES! OPPORTUNITIES?

MANY TIMES YES!') However, I think that it is not the war that makes this region attractive to missionaries so much as the character of the Montagnards. For nearly two centuries evangelical Protestants have tried, almost entirely in vain, to win converts from Hindus, Muslims, Buddhists, Jews and animists of the world. Even in Africa, where pagans were most amenable to a religious creed, the Protestants won fewer converts than did the Catholics or the Muslims. The most famous of all Protestant missionaries, David Livingstone, made only one convert, who afterwards back-slid. Because of this failure among the masses of Africa, China and India, the Protestants now focus their energies upon primitive peoples, the Highlands of Papua and New Guinea, which were not fully explored until after the Second World War, and have since been overrun by a number of bigoted, eager and mutually jealous missions engaged in the scramble for souls.

In contrast to the Protestants, Catholic missionaries have always concentrated their efforts, not on the most primitive but the most intelligent and advanced people in any tropical region. In Africa they had most success with the Ibos and the Baganda, while in Asia, long before French rule, they won many converts among the Vietnamese. Although the South Vietnamese Catholics number less than ten per cent of the population, they have disproportionate influence in the army, the civil service, parliament and in certain geographical regions, notably the Highlands. Many Catholics from the north were settled here during the rule of Diem, himself a Catholic with a fierce and eventually fatal missionary zeal. Even today the Catholic Church identifies with the Vietnamese and has made few conversions among the Montagnards, whom it considers too steeped in superstition to grasp the reality of the Faith. Individual priests have hinted to me that most conversions claimed by the Protestants are founded on ignorance and revivalist hysteria.

Although a believer in neither faith, I find Catholic priests

easier company than ministers of the more fervent Protestant
sects. The Alliance missionaries, although kind and hospitable,
were disconcertingly personal in their relations with the Deity.
I could not get used to His constant supervision of life at
Dalat: 'We'll leave at nine if the Lord gives us the car back
from the garage.' 'The road should be all right, for the Lord
gives us good weather on Sunday'. 'I had a temperature after
tennis but the Lord heard our prayers and two hours later I was
playing chess.' When I went with them to Christian Montagnard villages to drink lemonade with suited men in cement-
floored, tin-roofed bungalows, I thought wistfully of other days
spent in pagan Montagnard villages, where we drank rice wine
in a thatched, wooden long-house with men and women
wearing only sarongs.

This trip being made on a Sunday, we set out early enough
to attend a church service at Khut, about thirty miles south-west
of Dalat. The driver was Helen Evans and the other missionary
David Heath was a tall, straight-backed and earnest Englishman in his twenties who told me that he had served as a policeman in Leicestershire, and had hunted with the Quorn. As
we drove, Miss Evans pointed out places of sacred interest such
as the villages which had been 'dealt with by the Lord', and a
clump of sacred bamboo of which the pagans had lived in fear
until the Christians built their church right beside it. We
slowed up at the sight of a man in the road on his stomach,
reading a newspaper, at which I attempted a joke about how it
was just like England, where everyone lazed about with the
Sunday papers, I raised no laughs. These were not, I remembered too late, the sort of people who lie about reading the
Sunday Times until the pubs open.

The church at Khut had been burned down by the Communists five years before but rebuilt with a blood-red cross
over the door. There are 150 Protestants in this village of 2,000
people, most of whom had been moved here from the hills
round about. Most of the faithful, most of whom were young

children, had joined the congregation that morning, in spite of
the fact that services last for an hour and a half. It should be
said that, as church services go, this was good entertainment,
with many hymns, a choral octet and plenty of jokes in the
sermons, if that is the word. A young man in a blue shirt
and tight, flared trousers warned us against drink: 'I don't
know how many people here drink wine, but you should fill
yourself with holy spirit. You think too much of feasts and
gongs.' Another man from Dalat said that life without love
was like the dummy of Lincoln at Disneyland in Los Angeles,
which spoke the Gettysburg address on tape.

About half way through the service, some firing began in the
hills to the west—an artillery strike, so I was afterwards told—
and a mouse scuttled out from behind the dais, much to the
concern of the minister. These events came before what was to
me the star turn of the service, the testimony of David Heath,
translated by Helen Evans. He stood at ease, dressed in a neat
blue suit, looking much as he once must have looked giving
evidence in a Leicestershire magistrate's court as he told how
he had given up beer and cigarettes and turned to Christ, while
the brown congregation listened entranced, the artillery
boomed, the mouse scuttled to and fro, and the pagans
smoked cigarettes outside in the street of this village eight
thousand miles from Leicestershire.

Ban Me Thuot

Since the Alliance missionaries are an evangelical sect, they
spend much of their time producing local translations of the
Bible, the whole Bible, a book I have always thought would
benefit by abridgement. 'We normally start with St Mark
because it's the shortest and most narrative,' I was told by
Helen Evans, 'and much more easy to understand than for
instance St. John.' There are now translations of Mark in

seventeen Montagnard languages, with one on the way in
Cham, an astonishing tribute to the industry of the translators.
When I first went to Ban Me Thuot, in the western highlands,
the missionaries still had not finished translating the Bible into
Rhadé, the language of the local tribe which is the largest in
South Vietnam. An Alliance missionary, Donald Ziemer, explained to me (this was in 1967) that when he had first arrived,
twenty years earlier, they had had to make do with St Mark in
mimeograph, and it had taken him all that time to translate
the New Testament and the Psalms. He explained to me, and
Helen Evans confirmed, the enduring difficulty of avoiding
linguistic confusion between Christ's sacrifice on the cross
and the Montagnard word for sacrifice, which means killing
an animal with a blunt instrument. But Zirmer was pleased to
find that the Rhadé had learned a sense of sin. 'My predecessor
said to me: "You will find the people here will not weep over
their sins." But I've lived to see it. Now they weep.' A few
months later, in January 1968, Ziemer was one of the six
American missionaries at Ban Me Thuot to be shot to death
by the Communists. The whole mission was trapped by
Communist troops when Ziemer came out of cover shouting
'We are civilians, with women and children' and took a burst of
shots in the chest. However Ziemer's life work had not been
in vain, for his successor Phil Young told me four years later
that they had now completed a full translation of the Rhadé
Old Testament. 'Providentially, only one of the manuscripts was
lost at Tet.'

As the massacre of the missionaries showed, this western
part of the highlands has always been more violent than the
east, with greater suffering for the Montagnards as a con-
sequence. For years there has been constant fighting in Pleiku
and Kontum provinces, north of Darlac, and in the eastern
or highland part of the provinces still further north. By the
time of the cease-fire in 1973 virtually all this region was ruled
by the Communists. Those Montagnards who stayed in

Refugee child with copy of 'Playboy'.
(*Previous page*). *Eleven year old Vietnamese soldier.*

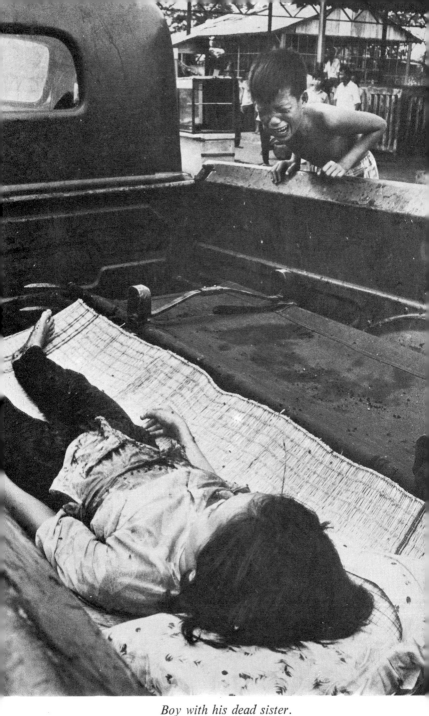

Boy with his dead sister.
Killed by US helicopter gunship during May offensive 1968.

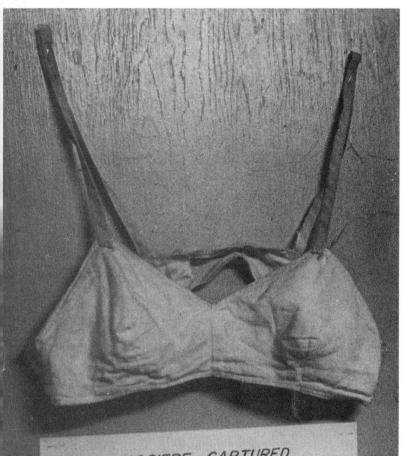

VC BRASSIERE CAPTURED
BEHIND TAN DINH ISLAND
BY RIVER DIVISION 51
15 SEPTEMBER 1967

Bar in Nha Trang.
(Previous page). View across the river in Saigon.

Communist territory have had to endure years of intense bombing; those that fled faced years in a refugee camp. In disputed areas or those controlled by Saigon, tens of thousands of Montagnards have been forcibly 'relocated' and seen their land given to carpet-bagging Vietnamese. The relocation process reached its climax in 1971 under the supervision of General Dzu, Commander of II Corps. A darling of the Americans (until he became too involved in the heroin traffic), Dzu believed in the Hamlet Evaluation System (or HES), which classified every village in South Vietnam by degree of government control. An 'A' village, for instance, was totally controlled, a 'D' village was scarcely controlled and a 'V' village was held by the Viet Cong. When Dzu came to II Corps he was appalled by the number of 'C', 'D' and 'V' villages, which he rightly assumed were providing food, shelter and new recruits for the Communists. Rather than trying to win over the hostile or dissident villages, Dzu simply removed them. The missionary Phil Young told me of the methods used in relocation. 'Sometimes the Vietnamese gave them sufficient warning in advance. Sometimes they just arrived by chopper and told them to be ready to leave in two or three hours' time. Then they destroyed the houses, killed the livestock and poisoned the crops.'

The relocations improved Dzu's rating by HES. 'We've just heard from Nha Trang,' he crowed to a colleague in 1971, 'and we're now rated second in pacification on the HES. When I took over II Corps we were rated the lowest of all the four corps.' Not only was this achievement worthless, for the HES ratings were as spurious as the information on which they were based, but relocation brought misery to the Montagnards. Deprived of their rice lands, their livestock, poultry and game, they could not stomach the foreign foods they were offered in the resettlement camps. Accustomed to cool, wooden longhouses, they felt hot and miserable in tin-roofed, concrete huts. Forbidden their sacrifices, their rice-wine feasts and their gongs, they became morose and begged from the Vietnamese to buy cheap alcohol from the Vietnamese shopkeepers.

The plight of the Montagnards shocked some US officials, who claimed in a report of March 1971 that children in the resettlement camps were dying of malnutrition and diarrhoea. They reported from 214 to 260 deaths at Plei to Ko Tu camp and 36 at Plei Pang Da, but this news was eclipsed by the more exciting charges against General Dzu of smuggling heroin from the country.

Meanwhile the Vietnamese population in the highlands rose from 20,000 in 1954 to well over half a million today. In Darlac province the 100,000 Vietnamese now outnumber the Montagnards, whose land has been seized and who have to do labouring jobs such as constructing camps for themselves. The pillage has been disguised by a pretentious show of affection for the Montagnards on the part of the Saigon Vietnamese. President Nguyen Van Thieu, in 1971, made a much-publicised trip to Pleiku, where he donned a Montagnard costume and greeted carefully chosen chiefs. It was arranged that a buffalo should be sacrificed in his honour and its blood poured over his feet in time-honoured fashion, but on the day Thieu's staff advised that a sacrifice filmed for TV might give offence to American lovers of animals, so the buffalo was pre-killed and Thieu's feet anointed with wine.

The Americans who remain as advisers or consular staff have lost their romantic affection for the Montagnard way of life. They are a different species from Mike Benge, who was here in the early Sixties and lived most of the time in a long-house. At Tet 1968 he was taken prisoner by the Communists and not released until 1972, during which four years of privation and suffering the Montagnards whom he had helped were being destroyed. At Mike Benge's house in 1967 an American AID official said to me: 'If the Montagnards don't modernise, the same thing's going to happen to them that happened to the American Indian. They're going to be killed off or debased or locked up in a reservation.' The AID man and Mike Benge were trying to modernise the Montagnards by getting them to make carvings for the commercial market—cute Disney-like cats and elephants. Then Benge went into captivity and the AID man became a successful diplomat and the Montagnards were killed off or debased or locked up in a reservation.

By 1971 even the US aid officials had grown indifferent to the plight of the Montagnard. The first two I approached refused to talk to a journalist, but I found a third in the bar of the Chinese hotel. He was ready to talk when I said that I too liked Kipling, his favourite poet, although he ignored Kipling's appeal to America to take up the white man's burden. He was only too eager to let the burden drop. 'The Montagnards in these camps are eating the bark off the trees,' he said. 'Of course they've always eaten bark but we should give them better bark before putting them onto something more nutritious. Instead we give them a few thousand pounds of Bulga flour and cooking oil and we think how generous we've been. It's like the American Indians. But do you really care what happens to these people? Aren't you really only interested in yourself, your family?' He bought two more beers, recited the *Road to Mandalay* and nodded towards a bar girl who was sitting on my left. 'She's lovely, really beautiful, isn't she? It's kind of sad to think that in a year or so she may be marched through the street with her head shaved.'

One loyal friend of the Montagnards is an Italian coffee planter, Santilli, whose name is legendary in the central highlands. Since he lives more than ten miles from Ban Me Thuot and comes into town only a few times each month, it was not till my fourth visit that I met the famous Italian in the no less famous café La Souris Blanche. He turned out to be a stocky, ruddy-faced man of about sixty with lively, brown eyes, a loud voice, still louder check shirt and a soft white hat on his head. He was teasing an old priest in an argument interspersed by fake tantrums of fury: 'You should have a woman, *mon père*, it's ridiculous that you don't have a woman.' 'At my age?' the priest rapped back, and started to sulk over his vermouth. I went to Signor Santilli and showed him a letter of introduction from M. Ottavj, the proprietor of the Royal Hotel where Santilli stays when in Saigon. He promptly asked me to come out to lunch with him at his plantation. The drive was noisy, for Signor Santilli is an Archangel Gabriel on the car horn, and it was also slow, for he kept stopping to talk with friends, doffing his hat to the men and ogling the women, especially the Montagnard girls. As we passed the coffee plantations he pointed out with bellows of indignation where Vietnamese had taken the land—'not bought, *taken*, Monsieur!'—until we came to his own wooden house, perched on stilts in a clearing. We drank aperitifs on the veranda looking down on a hillside of gum trees, bare and ghastly white, rising tall as a cathedral out of the underbrush from which came spicy smells and the noise of crickets. His Montagnard wife and their several beautiful daughters served us and the other guests by far the largest meal I have ever consumed in the tropics. Parma ham was followed by paté, spaghetti, steak, cheese and papaya doused with cognac that supplemented the vermouth, red wine and champagne.

'The VC often come through here,' said Signor Santilli over the coffee, 'they were here last night, although only in small numbers. After Tet 1968 the Americans dropped a stick of napalm on my plantation, destroying 22 hectares, but what can you expect in a war?' Yet the plantation appeared a peaceful, even a happy place as we went for a tour in the afternoon. 'All my employees are Montagnards,' Signor Santilli said, 'and I pay them well on piece rate, so that they work as much as they want. They're very good people.' It was clear that the plantation workers returned M. Santilli's affection, as well as the bawdy shouts and the mock abuse that he roared at them in the Rhadé tongue. It was December, the start of the coffee harvest, and as we moved through the dark, green bushes we came upon groups of Montagnard girls, picking and sorting the green from the red beans. My host made a pounce on many girls, who screamed, ran away, laughed or in one case bared her behind in derision. These girls must have escaped so far from the Protestant missionaries, for they had not learned 'to weep for their sins' or to read the works of Homer H. Dowdy.

Signor Santilli's attitude to the Montagnards would not appear to be based on liberal ideology. Later that day, when we were once more on his verandah drinking beer, I saw him get out a gramophone and a record, so that soon the forest was sounding to the swell of Italian oratory: '*Italiani*! *L'Italia ha finalmente l'impero*! *L'impero fascista*!' It was Mussolini, on 9 May 1936, announcing his African victory with the capture of Addis Ababa.

Nha Trang

Some Montagnard tribes believe that their ancestors lived on the coast, by modern Nha Trang, from which they were driven westwards into the mountains. The legend may well be true of the Polynesian tribes, in which case it is appropriate that Nha Trang was base for the American Special Forces, or Green Berets, who befriended and took up the cause of the Montagnards. The rise and fall of this famous regiment was important not just to the Montagnards but to the history of the war and even to the history of the Americans, who lost with the Green Berets some of their old faith in themselves.

The Green Berets had been formed on the assumption that anything the Communists did the Americans could do better; they would be better jungle guerilla fighters, more courageous, more ingenious, more popular with the Vietnamese and above all inspired by a better ideology of liberty, democracy and free enterprise. The Green Berets were identified in the public mind with the classic American heroes and frontiersmen, with Davy Crockett, with Gary Cooper in *High Noon*, with John Wayne in *Stagecoach*. They were the only American troops in the war to be objects of glamour and to inspire a best-selling novel, a famous song and a Hollywood epic, all titled 'The Green Berets'. The myth of the Green Berets was to vanish in dis-illusionment, but before that time its influence was immense, particularly on the Americans who served in Vietnam. The novel, which must have been read by hundreds of thousands of servicemen, offered a neat kit of received ideas concerning the war, the Communists, ARVIN, the French, the Montagnards and such delicate moral issues as the torturing of prisoners. Many times in Vietnam I have heard incidents from the novel repeated as recent fact and I have even read them as news in the local press.

The fame of the Special Forces was still more remarkable since they were formed, in 1952, as a secret military arm of the CIA. Unconventional troops had been used by the Allies in World War II, proving successful in Burma, but the undoubted master of military dirty tricks was Otto Skorzeny, the German general and kidnapper of Mussolini. During the Battle of the Ardennes, Skorzeny dressed some of his men as American military policemen and sent them behind the opposing lines to snarl up traffic. This cheeky prank impressed even its vic-tims, who liked to dream up similar tricks in Vietnam. Al-though ex-Nazis were not allowed in the Special Forces, many recruits were East European refugees, who were trained as potential guerillas behind the Iron Curtain. Fluency in a foreign language was just as essential as parachute-jumping to qualify for a green beret, although both were useless in Vietnam where parachutists put down from helicopters and Polish-speakers wasted their skill on the Vietnamese and the Montag-nards.

The Special Forces have been employed in Korea, Germany, Latin America, Ethiopia, and above all, Indo-China. They first came to Vietnam during the rule of Ngo Dinh Diem, who was to be murdered after a coup ordered by John F. Kennedy, only a few days before Kennedy's own murder on 22 November

1963. Since American troops then served in an advisory capacity, each 12-man 'A' Team, under a captain, was technically answerable to a Vietnamese counterpart, but it could recruit and command a 'civilian irregular force defence group' almost invariably from the Montagnards or the Cambodian minority. This hiring of non-Vietnamese to defend Vietnam was not as absurd as it sounds, since the Green Berets were mostly deployed in the highlands and frontier areas, as distinct from the coastal strip. Most of the population in this region were Montagnards, Cambodian or followers of the Cao Dai and Hoa Hao, two Vietnamese religious groups that were cool to the Saigon government. Inevitably this arrangement caused bitterness between the Green Berets and their counterparts in the Vietnamese army. Nevertheless it seemed to the US government of the time that friction with Saigon was tolerable as a price for a string of Green Beret 'A' Teams, each with its band of mercenaries, to guard the cities and rice paddies of coastal Vietnam. When in 1961 a jealous American general tried to ban the symbolic green beret, President Kennedy cancelled the order and urged the Special Forces to wear the headgear with pride as 'a trade mark of distinction and a badge of courage in the difficult days ahead'.

That it became so was largely due to the author and journalist Robin Moore, who wrote the best-selling novel *The Green Beret*. The idea for this came to him while he was writing a book about counter-insurgency in the Caribbean. He approached the then Vice-President Johnson, who was visiting Jamaica, and through him was offered assistance in his research, provided he took the whole Special Forces training course of parachute-jumping, jungle manoeuvres, unarmed combat and armed combat with gun, crossbow, longbow and garotte. Having passed the course and received his wings, quite an achievement for a man in his late thirties, Moore went to Vietnam to spend six months with various 'A' Teams, taking part in their many engagements. The fact that Moore

was befriended and given a green beret by the men he had come
to observe lends authority to his published account which,
unhappily, had to be fictionalised for reasons of security.
'You will find in these pages many things that you will find hard
to believe,' Moore wrote in a preface. 'Believe them. They
happened this way. I changed details and names but I did not
change the basic truth.' This fictional treatment also allowed
Moore to trim and tidy the 'basic truth' of the novel, giving
the anecdotes a neatness seldom found in real life but always
found in the strip cartoon, the TV serial and the 'flaming,
block-buster best-seller', as Moore's book is described on the
blurb. Like the Montagnard Christians in Homer H. Dowdy's
book, the Green Berets always come out on top of the Communists, except when betrayed by back-sliding or cowardly
allies. We hear nothing of set-backs or blunders, which leads
us to wonder how much of the 'basic truth' is also historical
truth. But before I discuss its implications, I should describe
the book, which may not have stuck in the memory even of
those who read it ten years ago. Indeed so great is the change
since then in our attitude to Vietnam, that *The Green Berets* has
a period flavour, as though of some earlier war—like gas-masks,
ration books or posters of Churchill and Stalin embracing at
Yalta.

The hero of the first tale in the book is a gigantic Finn,
Captain Kornie, who has to defend his camp not only against
the Communists but the perfidy of his own side. 'By God damn!
Those Vietnamese generals—stupid. Two hundred fifty my
best men that sneak-eyed yellow-skin bastard corps commander
take out of here yesterday—and our big American generals!
Politics they play while this camp gets zapped!' Captain Kornie
is particularly annoyed that he is not allowed to chase the
Communists into neutral Cambodia, a prohibition he cir-
cumvents by hiring bandits to cross the border. They find a
VC infiltrator whom they interrogate by driving a long, heavy
pin into his thumb, thereby forcing him to reveal that the camp

is due for attack the next evening. The narrator is asked by Captain Kornie, over a schnapps, what he thinks of this style of interrogation. 'It's always grim', the narrator replies, 'but I've been around some damned crude sessions.' Two nights later the camp fights off an attack by human waves of hate-filled, fanatic VC.

In another story an 'A' Team sets out to kidnap a VC colonel called Ling, whose concrete and stone headquarters are deep in the jungle and evidently immune from air attack. Some of Ling's men raid a government hamlet whose chief and his family they disembowel, leaving the pigs to eat the guts. A Green Beret intelligence sergeant takes photographs of this atrocity, then traces the hamlet chief's daughter to Saigon. He shows her the photographs—'he knew the moment for the necessary brutality had arrived'—and later persuades her to act as decoy for General Ling. She gets a cover job in the district as teacher at the Americans' school, meets Colonel Ling and agrees to become his mistress provided he comes into town, where the kidnap can be affected. However, she tells the sergeant, she will not go ahead with the operation unless she is sure that it does not make her pregnant by a Communist. The account of how a Dutch cap is procured and then fitted into the girl by a Green Beret man is treated with long and leering facetiousness.

One incident takes place in Laos which at that time, 1964, was enjoying a peace agreed by the big powers. However, as Moore rightly says, the Communist Vietnamese were using the eastern part of the country as a sanctuary and a supply base for their men in South Vietnam. The American State Department and even the Army were shutting their eyes to this fact for fear of breaking the truce and the peace in Laos; but the CIA, according to Moore, was anxious to launch an attack on the Communist infiltrators. In Moore's story a Special Forces officer employed by the CIA befriends a tribe of the Montagnard Meo and trains them for an assault on the Communists.

Although having 'slight trepidations' about firing the first shots in a new war in Laos, he mounts an ambush that kills almost a company of Communists.

Did that incident really happen? And did the CIA really parachute into North Vietnam a group of Green Berets who kidnapped a province chief and blew up a bridge and power station? If such an operation really took place one might have thought that the Americans would have sent Vietnamese troops to infiltrate the northern part of their country. But according to Moore only one Vietnamese took part in an operation performed by non-Caucasian Americans such as Negroes, Filipinos and Arabs who passed themselves off as Montagnards. If these men were captured, according to Moore, the North could not blame the Americans for the attack. I find it hard to believe that even the CIA could think up quite such a fat-headed and dangerous plan, but in the book, needless to say, the raid is wholly successful and presages further raids that will bring 'a shaken, fearful Hanoi' to the conference table.

The exciting narrative of the book is not for a moment held up by political speculation. We read of Communist human waves, we are told that at one plantation most of the tappers are Communists, but we are never asked to reflect why these people gained their conviction. We get the impression that most of the South Vietnamese are venal cowards who take a delight in torturing prisoners (in contrast to the Americans, who do not enjoy it) but we are not encouraged to ask why they resent the optimistic and well-paid Special Forces. Still less are we led to inquire why America should support such an apparently rotten regime.

The foulest villains of Moore's book are the French, whose President Charles de Gaulle had offended America in the early Sixties. I was startled to read as 'basic truth' that most French rubber planters were Communist sympathisers, that French hotels such as the Continental paid VC tax, and that one of the VC's officers was a huge Frenchman who went into battle stripped to the waist, wearing levis and cowboy boots. This startling character first appears at the Cercle Sportif in Saigon and last appears bleeding to death in a tea plantation, 'barely identifiable as a Caucasian now except for his great size'. The book must have contributed to the widespread hatred felt for the French by American troops and civilians, few of whom probably talked with or even saw a Frenchman. It must also have contributed to the recurring stories of VC troops led by a giant Caucasian, sometimes a Frenchman, sometimes a US deserter and sometimes a Russian, but never, to my knowledge killed, wounded or captured.*

The admirable characters in this book, after the Green Berets themselves, are the Montagnards from the Meo, Tai, Bru and Katu tribes, who appear as loyal, humorous, trusting and anti-communist. They look to the Americans for protection against the South Vietnamese, who call them savages, bomb their villages and deny them medical treatment. In *The Green Berets* Moore accepts some of the Montagnard customs that are denounced in *The Bamboo Cross* by his fellow American, Homer H. Dowdy. Their feasts of rice wine give the Montagnards courage to fight; their ignorance makes them proof against communist dogma; their voluptuous women, in two of the stories, bed down with Special Forces men. In view of Moore's national prejudice, it is curious to remark that in both cases the girls are half-castes, fathered by French soldiers in an earlier war. Perhaps an affair with a pure brown Montagnard would have made the book unacceptable in the southern states and the useful South African market.

It is a constant refrain of *The Green Berets* that 'the guy in the field' who is 'fighting the war to win' could soon smash the Communists if he was not held back by cowardly politicians. In particular they were held back from attack on North Vietnam, from pursuit of Communists into Cambodia and

* The few Caucasians who appeared in VC districts were East European reporters and TV crewmen.

from cutting the Ho Chinh Minh Trail through Laos. After the book came out the Americans changed their policy, unloosing large-scale attacks on all three countries, in each case with brutal but unsuccessful results. If Special Forces men were dropped into North Vietnam, as described by Moore in his book published in 1965, their raids cannot have proved effective. That very year the United States began six years of obliteration bombing that still did not break the fighting will of the North, still less—to recall Moore's phrase—bring 'a shaken, fearful Hanoi' to the conference table. Like Moore, the American leaders never allowed for the strength of communist ideology. Like Moore, they believed that Laos and Cambodia would side with them in hostility to the communist Vietnamese. As a result of US attacks on Laos and Cambodia, both countries are now largely controlled by their own native Communists under the tutelage of the North Vietnamese, whose line of supply to the south carries ever-increasing traffic. The policy of 'fighting the war to win' achieved little apart from the death of some million, mostly civilian Vietnamese, Laotians and Cambodians. Those Meo tribesmen who trusted the Green Berets were rendered almost extinct as a reward.

I have remarked on Moore's casual assumption that torture is necessary as a means of obtaining intelligence. The huge sale of his book, especially to troops in Vietnam, certainly helped to endorse this view and to make torture respectable. In 1966, before the Americans set up torture squads to interrogate prisoners, they were woefully inefficient in normal intelligence methods. During one operation a colonel complained to me that the other side kept one jump ahead by listening in to the American radio messages. When I asked if it was not possible to listen to the Communists' messages, he replied: 'Yes. But they have people who understand English. We don't have anyone who understands Vietnamese.' But the use of torture as a means of gaining intelligence is unreliable and, in this kind of war, self-defeating. Fear of torture discouraged

Communists from defecting, steeled them against surrender and fostered a savage hatred of the Americans and their allies. As revolutionaries have discovered from Yugoslavia to Algeria to Cuba, the use of torture and violence by an oppressive regime actually wins recruits to the guerilla forces. This is especially true in countries such as Algeria or Vietnam, where foreigners of a different race employ the torture.

The blurb of my copy compares *The Green Berets* for excitement with Ian Fleming's James Bond spy thrillers, which sold in millions during the Sixties. Certainly Bond is ruthless, violent and obsessed with torture, although I suspect more masochist than sadist—the upper-class Englishman who enjoyed his nanny's spankings. Like Moore's heroes, Bond seems to have no thought-processes outside his work. He never opens a book, or argues, or questions what he is doing. On the other hand he is much excited by all kinds of machine and technological gadget, such as eaves-dropping equipment, magnetic wrist-watches, explosive triggers, and above all guns. The Green Berets in the book are obsessed by firearms, and in real life I have frequently seen one of them strip, oil, clean, fondle and play with a gun to the point of obscenity and embarrassment. Like Bond, the Green Berets were excited by flying and jumping out of and into all kinds of helicopters and aeroplanes, but there the resemblance ends, for the James Bond books were redeemed and indeed made enjoyable by Fleming's wit and an element of self-parody, while Moore and his Green Berets are in deep earnest.

The earnestness of this book served to influence as well as express American attitudes to Vietnam in the first half of the Sixties. It was the age of President Kennedy, with his half-baked rhetoric of the New Frontier, the Peace Corps, the Alliance for Progress and other slogans dreamed up by bad dons and Madison Avenue copy-writers. The man who admired James Bond and the Special Forces would surely have liked *The Green Berets*, with its frontiersman derring-do, its patriotism, its optimism, its action, its speedy results. President Kennedy made on an international scale the same mistakes made by the Green Berets in the jungles of Vietnam. Unable or unwilling to understand the Communists, he fought their ideology with technology. An optimist and an entrepreneur, he valued reflection less than action, and when action failed he resorted to mere motion: hence the constant photographs of him with aides or his family moving from plane to helicopter to car to boat. This restlessness, this idea that thought matters less than action, and action less than motion, cursed Kennedy's two inheritors of the war in Vietnam. President Johnson, who liked to drink beer while driving at 100 miles per hour, first lit on the idea that Vietnam would be more comprehensible if he went there. He would go all the way to the Philippines, then fly on a surprise two-hour visit to Cam Ranh Bay, the only air base in Vietnam considered secure enough for a President. But it was secure because it was totally American, and not therefore the place to learn about Vietnam. President Nixon, so one reads in the newspapers, has become so afflicted with motion mania that he spends his time on almost continual trips from Washington to Camp David to Los Angeles to Miami.

By the time of Nixon's presidency the Green Berets were discredited and were soon to be pulled out of the war. As Robin Moore warned in his book there was much hostility to the Green Berets from officers who wanted a more conventional war, with large units and good possibilities of promotion. Both officers and men in the infantry and Marines resented the cult of the Green Berets, whom they accused of braggadocio and conceit. Even in 1967, two years after Moore's book was published, the Special Forces were far from the supermen he described. In one 'A' Team with whom I stayed for a week at least three of the men were fat, dull and idle, with no apparent interest in fighting the local Communists. Everyone in the mess except myself and the photographer suffered from stomach pains which were blamed on the water. The more they suffered the more disinfectant they put in the water, and the more they grew ill from the chemical. I grew friendly with one of the officers, a man from the forests of south Illinois, who at last said out loud what I knew he had been thinking: 'The brass are trying to get rid of us. LBJ doesn't like us and nor does the other Johnson, the Chief of Staff. What they're doing is filling up the 'A' teams with men from other regiments. Most of them haven't jumped, some are no good at all.' He nodded towards the camp and I knew what he meant. In Moore's book the Special Forces were secretive with outsiders and in particular did not voice the resentment they felt against the LLDB, their South Vietnamese opposite numbers. 'It is important to understand,' wrote Moore, 'that Special Forces men do not comment on their counterparts to the outside world. Only after I became one of them did they talk freely to me.' On the contrary, I found most of the Green Berets only too eager to talk. One captain, met by chance in a bar, told me about a forthcoming march through Laos to North Vietnam and then inquired casually if I would like to come too. (I remembered a previous engagement.) As for the LLDB, Special Forces men seldom failed to point out that the letters stood for 'Lousy Little Dirty Bastard', a joke that appears in Moore's book as 'Lousy little dirty bug-outs'. Most of them had enjoyed the book, and still more, the stirring if mournful song, which I have heard a dozen times in a row on a Special Forces juke-box. I have seen Green Beret men poring over the weekly *Green Beret* comic book, which was sold by the hundreds at PX stores. The cover of one shows an imperilled and half-naked white woman, with underneath the caption: 'Nothing stood between the reds and Saigon, thirty miles away—except a handful of Green Berets.'

I met one Special Forces commander as daring and dashing as those in the book, but he was also a psychopath and a mass murderer, of whom I would say more but for legal reasons. In the end an illegal killing performed by a Green Beret officer provided the Saigon command with a pretext to close down this force. It came out that a Vietnamese double agent, discovered to be a Communist, had been killed, or to use the words of the Green Berets, 'terminated with extreme prejudice', which in this case meant being thrown from an aircraft into the sea off Nhatrang.

The Special Forces were on their way out when the film of *The Green Berets* came to Vietnam. Its star was the great western actor John Wayne, now paunchy and slow but with no less pugnacity in his sardonic snarl, and no less authority as the greatest Hollywood frontiersman. Moreover, as a political right-winger, Wayne threw his conviction as well as his skill into this role of a US officer. It is years since I saw the film, but some passages stuck in my mind and gave me much pleasure. There was the seduction of Colonel Ling, who goes by chauffeur-driven staff car to his mansion where he and his girl sit down to caviar and champagne. Since the location shots were done in America and no attempt was made to give authenticity to the background, the Vietnamese parts were performed by Chinese, Filipinos or even Japanese; the girls wore Chinese cheong-sams instead of the Vietnamese *ao dais*; rick-shaw men rather than cyclo-men scurried around Danang. This caricature of a country so well known and so much filmed must surely imply a deliberate flight from reality. Customers would not pay to see the depressing Vietnam of bombs and corpses and screaming babies, so Hollywood recruited its old papier-maché dream Far East and called it Danang or the central highlands. To help with publicity after the film was made, Wayne went to Vietnam to be photographed with some troops in the field. Shots were heard from the VC (or the publicity men) and afterwards Wayne gave each of the men a cigarette case inscribed with his signature and the words 'Fuck Communism'.

Early in 1969 I happened to meet a civilian in the United Services Organisation, which handled the distribution of films to the troops. I asked how the troops had enjoyed *The Green Berets*, which had then been in the country some weeks. 'They loved it,' he said. 'It's the biggest success we've ever had. They see it for laughs, you realise. There's one infantry unit just north of here where they've asked to see it three or four times. The bit they really love is where the helicopter is hit and bursts into flames at 3,000 feet and after that Wayne just steps out of the wreckage.' He said the Special Forces had liked the film but some, I hear, were very embarrassed.

At the end of his book Moore prophesied that whatever might happen in Vietnam, the Special Forces would 'continue to fight Communism and make friends for America in the under-developed nations that are the target of Communist expansion.' Yet in the highlands most of the old Special Forces camps have now been occupied by the Vietnamese of both sides, and the Montagnards, whom they befriended, are worse off than before. In Nhatrang, the former HQ, beggars patrol the beach and the bar girls are starving. 'That's my souvenir, do you want him?' a girl said, pointing towards her half-caste son, a wizened, autistic creature. At the Fregate Hotel, oysters are 25p a dozen and most of the guests are French, though not, I think, VC colonels on holiday from the interior.

Part Four
DELTA

After a bad day and a sleepless night I got up and walked down to the Saigon river to sit on a bench and meditate. By six o'clock there was a faint grey glow on the opposite bank, which is decorated with hoardings for Bastos cigarettes, the Japanese National TV company and Hynos, the Vietnamese toothpaste whose trademark is a grinning African. In Burma, according to Kipling, 'the dawn comes up like thunder, out'er China cross the bay', and I take people's word for it that the sun rises faster in the tropics; but not as fast as Kipling suggested. I waited till seven and it was still not day in Saigon.

Saigon is a great port, with ships always at anchor or moored near the heart of the city, so that on Navy Day you can inspect a fleet only a few hundred yards from the Royal Hotel. Nevertheless one is never aware of the river in Saigon as one is in Hue, Cairo, Budapest, London or Paris, where each bank has a separate character. The Saigon River is just an appendage to the town, an object of commerce rather than beauty, its waterfront blocked by a noisy main road. One of the first Americans to describe Saigon, a naval lieutenant who came here in 1820, was horrified by the squalor of the port and the inefficiency of the merchants. In recent years some attempt has been made to make the river attractive, or 'add to its amenities' in the modern jargon, but the result has been small. The floating restaurant was blown up by a bomb. The Thais, as part of some 'civic action' programme, provided a riverside children's playground but no traffic warden to guide the children across the murderous road.

Even at dawn there were many people beside the river. Two or three cyclo-drivers came to the dock to urinate; a Chinese, in white singlet and shorts, went by with the self-satisfied look of a man taking a constitutional; and half a dozen people were doing their morning exercises. I did not grasp at first what they were doing, for it was not what we would call physical jerks. First one man bent down as though to tie up his shoe-laces, then raised himself upright and stretched his arms sideways. Nearby a portly couple, in black pyjamas, lifted their arms slowly, with elbows bent, as if they were going to have their chest measurements taken, then dropped their arms and began again. None of these people, not even the husband-and-wife team, tried to co-ordinate their movements or put any effort into the job, but I noticed that all of them faced east to where the sky was turning a pale pink, barred by dark wisps of cloud. The callisthenics reminded me of the ritual practised by primitive tribes in New Guinea, who call on the sun each morning to rise and each day congratulate themselves on their prayers being answered. This morning in Saigon the sun first appeared just before seven, behind the National TV hoarding; on our side of the river, eight doves wheeled overhead and alighted beside a refuse bin.

The dawn reminded me that I had to make one more trip to the Mekong Delta, that complex of two rivers, many canals and rice paddies, with which Saigon is linked and from which it derives wealth and power. I had been putting off this journey for reasons of sloth, fear of road travel and a foreboding, soon proved correct, that I would not enjoy myself. In the time of the Americans, the dreariness of the Delta towns was offset by the attractiveness of the countryside, through which you could travel by boat past banana groves, houses on stilts, water buffaloes up to their neck in water, and multitudinous ducks. A friend of mine used to say that when the war was over he was going to hire a house-boat and cruise in the Delta from Vung Tau, south of Saigon, up to Phnom Penh. It remains an attractive idea but of course the war is not over and nowadays it is difficult for a foreigner in the Delta to get away from the main road. The journalist has to stay in one of the province towns and make his guesses, ever more feeble, about what the peasants are thinking or why the price of rice remains high. I can attempt only a side-swipe at both questions. Early in 1969, when the Americans were here, I spent a fortnight making a film at Xuan Dong, a village near My Tho, about forty miles south-west of Saigon. The experience taught me something about the Delta and rather more about the role of TV in presenting Vietnam to the world. On the day that I began by watching the dawn in Saigon I went back to My Tho and later to Can Tho, the capital of the Delta region, where I once more studied the problems of rice, the economy and capitalism in Vietnam.

My Tho

In London, in late 1968, I got a telephone call from the BBC saying that Richard Taylor, the TV director, wanted to talk to me about Vietnam. I asked around and learned that he was a very good director but I went to lunch in no spirit of expectation. Any free-lance journalist with the remotest claim to some special knowledge is used to having his brain picked by the television companies at a price ranging from £10 downwards to a free lunch or nothing at all. At one low point in my journalistic fortunes I spent four weeks in Addis Ababa, expecting to hear from a magazine with an assignment in East Africa. At six o'clock on the last day the hotel clerk told me that London was on the telephone and I ran to my room to take the call, only to find that although London could hear me, I could not hear them. Assuming that this was the magazine, I bellowed instructions for £300 in expenses, air tickets to Dar es Salaam and Kampala, and cabled instructions concerning the article. I put down the telephone and poured a

Scotch. When London came back on the line, very clear this time, it was a most polite if puzzled girl from the BBC, who apologised for the misunderstanding and then explained that she was doing research for a documentary on the South Pacific islands. Could I possibly give her the names of some people to meet in the New Hebrides? In a half-dozen such talks about TV programmes on Vietnam, I have hinted in vain that if my services were required for research or advice, I should appreciate a round ticket to Saigon, all expenses and a substantial fee. But from the start of lunch with Richard Taylor I saw that, this time, there might be money involved. He told me that he was planning to do a film that would dispense with a regular TV reporter and use instead one or more newspaper men with experience of Vietnam. What aspect of Vietnam did I think might make a particularly interesting TV film? I was about to answer 'The Montagnards' when I remembered that I had tried that idea on at least three other TV producers, so I started to sing the wonders of life in a Delta village. Richard asked me, delicately, what newspaper men might be suitable for the film and already in Vietnam, because his budget did not extend to an air ticket from London. I mentioned a few names and then let drop, I hope with delicacy, that I was going to be in Saigon on an assignment for a magazine. A few weeks later, when I was in Bangkok waiting for Bob Hope, I got Richard's offer to take part in his film, which was to begin with Peter Arnett of Associated Press describing the work of a combat reporter, followed by me in a Delta village and Mark Frankland of *The Observer* on life in Saigon. On 19 January 1969 Richard and I set off to the Delta to find a suitable village.

We decided to look in Dinh Thuong province, which is populous, close to Saigon and fairly evenly split between the Communists and the government. Moreover, having been there before, I could boast previous knowledge which actually turned out to be useful. The Tet and May offensives of 1968 had wrought considerable change on the Americans in this province. In 1967 they had told me that two thirds of the province was in the control of the Saigon government, but now their latest 'hamlet evaluation count' showed barely fifty per cent, a figure agreed by the chief US adviser. 'People ask us if we're making progress,' he told me. 'But are we supposed to be making progress? It's our duty to protect the government supporters, even if they are only a small majority.' Two years before I had been told that the VC spirit was broken, but now a political officer said: 'Quite frankly, we haven't cracked the nut of the VC'. American propaganda had made much of the high rate of *Chieu Hoi*, or VC defection, but even these figures appeared to be suspect in Dinh Thuong province. The *Chieu Hoi* adviser told me this time (1969) that defection figures were no higher than two years before; that almost all the defectors were low-grade men who had joined the VC at the time of the Tet offensive; that almost all of them came from two particular hamlets. He denied the stories spread from Saigon that the VC had been reinforced by North Vietnamese regular troops. 'There are reports,' he said, 'but I don't believe them. The morale of the VC is very high in this province. The VC don't have much difficulty in recruiting, but many villagers don't want to work for the main force (the regulars). They prefer to work as guerillas and tend the fields by day.'

Such gloomy talk surprised me, because for years I had been hearing from the Americans of their political victory in the Delta. It was still more surprising since Dinh Thuong was one of the three Delta provinces where the US Army and Navy sent in combat troops to support ARVIN. American tanks—I saw three in a row named Alcatraz, Assassin and Amputator—ground through the suburbs of My Tho between the monstrous hedgerows of barbed wire; naval vessels patrolled the river and the canals to 'police up' (meaning to fire on) suspicious sampans; the artillery of the nearby 9th Division pounded away at villages in the 'free-strike zone'. In spite of or maybe because of this US intervention, the Communists seemed to be gaining ground. Villages I had visited (and described in *Sketches from Vietnam*) were reckoned too dangerous to be visited without company-strength support. This presented us with the problem of choosing a village to film. If it was typical, that is contested by both sides in the war, the villagers would be hostile or scared in the presence of foreigners. If the village was friendly and pro-government, it would not be typical. For reasons of time, filming conditions and (in my own case) cowardice, we decided to film in a pro-government village and to balance out the politics in the commentary. The village we chose, Xuan Dong, was remarkable in the region for its physical beauty. The same could not be said for My Tho, our base for the next fortnight. The coming of American troops had brought the usual abundance of barbed wire, black-market stalls, whores, bars and hatred to what had once been a quiet provincial town. Our small hotel was full of Koreans—the scowling variety, not the smiling—who spent most of their time walking naked along the corridor, screaming abuse at the staff or, to judge by the noise, smashing the furniture with their fists. On the water-front street, an old hunchback had learned to cadge cigarettes with the new phrases 'Okay! Number One!' Café loudspeakers howled out the latest popular songs, which included one set to the accompaniment of revolver shots. Sometimes one heard real revolver shots. One night I saw a small child run over and killed by a US truck. When the mother complained, she was arrested by Vietnamese police for making a nuisance. All night My Tho shook to the roar of American guns.

Our village, Xuan Dong, is five miles from My Tho and lies on both sides of a deep canal joining the Mekong to Saigon. The 5,000 inhabitants, in seven hamlets, grow rice, coconuts, oranges and bananas which they send to market by water. About three fifths of them belong to the Catholic church which also owns half the land, to the great disgruntlement of the Buddhist minority. The church, or cathedral as it is grandly

called, dates back to 1866 or nearly a century after the founding
of the village, which has survived by conformity and conser-
vatism. One of the village elders who had spent fifteen years
as a soldier said: 'The French were very easy compared to the
Japanese, who were very strict. The Americans have done a
lot to help us get richer. We've heard about the Australians and
the Thais but we haven't seen them. The young people here are
not affected by the Americanisation you see in the cities, but
they do like to wear nice clothes and to watch television.
People here listen to news on the radio, not the government or
the Viet Cong but the BBC'. This was said not in flattery to
our TV team but as simple fact; the BBC was regarded in
Vietnam as the best source of news, even by Communists.
Because of the loyalty of the village most of its young men
stayed at home for their national service, to join in the local
Popular Force. These 120 troops were not impressive—one of
our escorts got tight at a wedding and marched with a sprig of
bougainvillea stuck in his carbine—but at least they were ready
to fight for their families, homes and ancestral shrines.

When the Japanese surrendered in 1945 the Viet Minh
started a youth group in Xuan Dong, but with the return of the
French next year these Communists gave in their arms or
joined the guerillas. 'From about 1960,' the headman told us,
'the Viet Cong began again and since then about 40 villagers
have joined them, although six of these left last Tet. In a big
granary, a few grains will fall through the floorboard, to feed
the rats.' However we learned next day that the largest hamlet
with more than a thousand inhabitants, was actually under VC
control by night. This hamlet was on the other side of a stream,
which you crossed by a greasy tree-trunk, and was indis-
tinguishable from the part of the village this side. We
called at one cottage to find an old lady of eighty and her
son-in-law, who told us: 'The VC don't come often, perhaps
every two months, but the adult men are frightened of being
caught and they cross the river every night. If the VC caught

me they would burn me alive or cut my throat.' The old lady told me: 'When the VC knock on the door, I have to open up very quick and then they look inside to see if there are any men in the house. They say "How do you do, madam" and leave.'

The VC are not always so gentle. In the 'secure' part of the village I met two sisters whose lives had been scarred by the politics of assassination. One of them, Vo Thi Kho, had been in the house two years ago when the VC killed her father and two of his friends with a fusillade of machine-gun fire. 'It was an experience I shall never forget,' she said, with typical Vietnamese understatement. She now kept a small shop selling sweets, biscuits, tinned meat and sardines, which provided her with sufficient income. Her younger sister, Vo Thi That, had been widowed at twenty, two years before, when the VC ambushed her husband. 'Remarriage for me is a bleak prospect,' she said, 'for only a poor man would marry a widow.' There are seventy war widows in Xuan Dong, not counting the widows of men killed by assassination or stray bullets and shells—which kill about one person a month. In the less secure hamlets of Xuan Dong, each hut has some primitive dug-out shelter lined with wood, a car door or flattened beer cans soldered together. One old lady showed me her protections against attack—a shelter the size of a bath-tub and a packet of pills for blood pressure.

If the VC came to the village by night, the day was left to visits from earnest US officials. Their work was performed under various titles—USAID, redevelopment, pacification, reconstruction—but always its aim was to help the peasants to help themselves and to make them impervious to communist propaganda. When I first went to the Delta these aid officials were eager and confident that they could change the peasants by teaching them the experience of America. Very many of them regarded the Vietnamese as a cup which could be emptied of one substance, communism, and refilled with capitalist democracy. By 1969, the US aid officials were still earnest and eager to help but not quite so confident of success.

The favourite programme this year was the Revolutionary Self-Help Project, but Xuan Dong also enjoyed an esoteric Self-Government Pilot Scheme. The Project and the Scheme sometimes came into conflict, as we were told by the Scheme's representative, John Dodson, who had been arguing with the Project man, John Robinson. 'The Self-Help Project involves no US spending but is designed to help the villagers to appreciate their own needs and then to get help from the Saigon government. A census is taken and the villagers learn what is needed. If they find there are few children at school they may set up an Education Sub-Committee. If there is hog cholera caused by inadequate vaccination, they may set up an animal husbandry sub-committee. Everything depends on whether the government will respond. . . .Gosh, if the US Navy wanted to, they could vaccinate all the hogs, but that isn't the point. We want the demand to come from below. . .Tom keeps saying to me "I don't see any *ce*ment", but I reckon that *ce*ment's just something you add water to to make concrete. The US Navy can build any amount of schools but I say that I want the people to build their own school, so that if the VC blow it up the people are going to say "That wasn't a government school, that was *our* school" and they're going to chase the VC out of the village. I want self-government to start from the bottom up. Whenever I see the members of the council I say to them: "I'm not here to teach you what to do. I'm not a Vietnamese. I don't look like you. I don't even speak your language. You've got to make your own decisions."'

I never quite understood the difference between the Self-Government Pilot Scheme and the Revolutionary Development Self-Help Project, but I dare say this will be explained by historians.

Historians should also be interested in two other programmes, more clandestine and political, that were active in the Delta at this time. The Revolutionary Development Scheme and Operation Phoenix had both been devised by the Americans on the principle that in order to fight the Communists one must borrow their tactics, their ruthlessness and even their style of dress. The 'RD Cadre Teams', which exist to this day, are groups of young men and women in black pyjamas who live in politically contested areas, serving as guards, policemen and advisers. Even the word 'cadre' was borrowed from the Viet Cong, who had borrowed it from the French, who are not sure what it means.* The cadre teams were employed by the Americans to conduct 'Operation Phoenix', which started in 1968 as a propaganda operation but soon turned into a programme of political assassination. Since Xuan Dong was classified as a 'secure' village it did not qualify for an RD Team or 'Operation Phoenix', although both were active in nearby villages. I visited some of these teams and went to the home of the Province RD director, a Major Thom, who showed me a photograph of himself shaking hands with President Nixon. This year, he explained they were conducting a new programme known as 'Accelerated Pacification', which meant that the RD teams spent less time in the village. I asked if this meant that the RD teams were at half strength, to which Major Thom replied by showing me a photograph of himself with Bernard Fall that would have been more impressive had the historian not been looking in the opposite direction. A few days later I met an American in the district town (there are four districts to each province) who gave me a better idea of the role of the RD cadres in Operation Phoenix. 'There are several agencies in this province engaged in going into VC areas and murdering people. It's called "eliminating the VC infrastructure". Hell, the other side do it too.'

After a week of research for this TV documentary, the camera and sound crew arrived for the actual filming. Since

---

* A 'cadre' is literally a frame. It came to have a meaning much like the English 'cell' or 'agent'.

dawn and dusk are the best times for colour film, we worked a long week and were tired enough to sleep at night in spite of the artillery of the 9th Division; but I did not enjoy my stint as a TV reporter. For someone who hates being photographed it is still worse to be filmed, particularly when one must talk as well. I was filmed with John Dodson at an animal husbandry sub-committee; I was tape-recorded with him, saying nothing of interest; I was filmed 'looking natural' at an RD Cadre puppet show in which VC officers in moustaches and beards belaboured each other over the head like Punch and Judy. I was filmed on the balcony of the Tokyo Hotel in My Tho, reciting a statement that started: 'Dusk on the Mekong River, the waterway that gives life and rice to the people of South Vietnam'—or some such twaddle. In fact it was dawn, but we said dusk as I was holding a can of beer to allay my stage-fright. Nevertheless I kept muffing my lines and as far as I can remember the sequence was not used in the film.

We were well received in the village and asked to so many lunches, feasts and rice-wine parties that I gained about half a stone in a fortnight, but the Province Chief and his US advisers were most unwilling to let us stay in the village at night. Surely, we argued, Xuan Dong was secure? Surely the VC knew we were British and would not harm us? And if they did, surely that was a risk we took on our own volition? At last we were given permission to stay in the village one night provided that ARVIN performed a sweep of the district beforehand and we were accompanied by a US official. The second condition annoyed us because we thought this man might be from the CIA and because he carried a gun in his luggage. We were all invited to stay in the house of the priest, and the village chief gave us a dinner beforehand of dried deer and shrimp crackers, chicken and lettuce, sweet potato and port and rice gin. After dinner we went to the square in front of the church where some of the villagers had assembled to watch TV on a set donated by the American government. Perhaps for our benefit, the set had been switched to the US services station and it was showing a documentary on a Los Angeles public relations man: 'Let's talk to a man who's engaged in selling things and selling people.' This was followed by the emetic comedian, Dean Martin, who leered into the camera and said: 'I didn't sleep a wink last night, my jockey shorts were on too tight.' The audience started to drift away and the US official said to me that many people were frightened to watch TV for fear of attracting a VC rocket attack. The village had gone to sleep by the time we retired to our rush mats in the house of the priest, who appeared in his night-shirt to give us a drink of whiskey. 'This village is safe,' he assured us, 'but if anything happens you climb up that ladder into the loft.'

Night in the Delta is louder than night in Saigon. There are natural sounds such as the trilling and twanging of crickets, and a noise rather like radio static, as though the jungle mimicked the civilised world. Birds call continually *took-took-took*, often ending on cracked or false notes. There are *plop* sounds of frogs diving, or carp rolling for oxygen on the surface of the ponds. There are warning sounds, given mostly by pigs, turkeys and dogs, of which the pigs are the noisiest—they must fight in their dreams—while the turkeys and dogs cry out only to other animals. There were also plenty of military sounds: the US artillery firing 'H and I', meaning 'harassment and interdiction'; distant bombs, less noise than physical tremor; the cough of mortars (everyone calls it a cough) and the clatter of sub-machine guns. When the Viet Cong were around, or were thought to be around, the noise of the war increased to Somme volume. Then there were signal sounds. The government troops signal by firing their carbines in single shots or in bursts of up to seven. Sometimes they bang gongs as a warning, and from half past four in the morning I heard a great honking of car horns, which was eerie, because there was no road or car where the noise came from.

Rivers and canals are the thoroughfares of the Mekong

Delta and by half past five one could hear the first putter of outboard motors that by mid-morning was to become the background noise of the region. At six the church bell clanged and the choristers, carrying flaming brands, made their way to the church through the coconut groves and over the monkey bridge. They doused the brands in a heap in front of the church and started to chant in nasal plainsong. Meanwhile the priest had furnished us with a breakfast of bacon, a whole roast chicken, lettuce, radishes and tomatoes, salami, bananas and oranges, toast and butter, coffee, rum, whisky and banana liqueur. The US official told us that he had 'thoroughly savoured' the experience of spending a night in the village but he had not slept a wink—although not, I suspect, for the same reason as Dean Martin.

Back in Saigon I taped my stumbling commentary for the film, which was shown in England that June. The direction and camera work was excellent, so that one got a true impression of what Vietnam was like, but I wonder how much one learned of the politics. My left-wing friends said I was too kind to the Americans; my non-political friends said I should stick to newspaper journalism; the manageress of my block of flats said I was very good but it must have been terrible having to see all those Biafran babies. When I next went to Saigon I was surprised to find myself if not famous, at least known by sight to many people I did not know. It turned out that the American government had been pleased by a film that was not actually hostile and had screened the thing at special showings for weeks on end. For the first and last time I was struck off the list of those with a 'negative publication pattern' and rated instead a friend of the United States.

My later fall from grace was due to an article in which I quoted two US intelligence officers who had been working in the Delta on the Phoenix programme. One of them told me (*New Statesman*, 25 February 1972): 'The myth of a pacified Delta is just that—a myth. Under the HES (Hamlet Evaluation

System) ours was 94 per cent pacified, but two thirds of it was controlled by the VC. The eight VC hamlets are just marked as "uninhabited" but they *are* inhabited. If they were classified they'd be marked as "V" and the Province Chief would lose his rating. This myth of the pacified Delta has been dogging me all the time I've been here. The District Chief was only interested in quiet, in stopping the guerillas. He wasn't interested in harming the political organisation which provided its bread. After all, some of the VC were his relatives. He knew the VC district chief very well. Once when I was new and eager I suggested we should go and find this man, meaning to kill him. The District Chief said, "Do you want to meet him? I'll take you to his house to introduce you".'

The other officer with Operation Phoenix said: 'When I arrived in the district I was given a list of 200 names of people who had to be killed. When I left after six months' (he resigned in disgust) 'we still hadn't killed anyone on the list. But we'd killed 260 other people—their relatives perhaps. Sometimes our people would bring in the ears. Sometimes they'd leave the bodies by the roadside for a few days.'

Thus mythology was reversed and the ashes rose from Phoenix.

Can Tho

One café beside the Mekong has a mural of three full-busted mermaids standing upon a shore and four more waving from the broad stream. As soon as I saw it I thought of the *Rheingold* and how I wished I was back in London to see all the *Ring*, until I recalled that it was not the season and anyway you can no longer get tickets for Wagner these days. Then I tried to remember the Rhine theme, which was impossible, as the whole café shook to the music of Vietnam's pop hero, Elvis Phuong. I therefore started to think about *Rheingold* as a

symbol of capitalism and whether that old thesis applied to
Vietnam. Alberich forswore love in order to steal the gold from
the Rhinemaidens; Wotan betrayed his godhood to steal the
ring and to build Valhalla; a warrior, Siegfried, was born to
protect the gold but was killed for it, as Valhalla burned and
was swept into the Rhine.

Just as the Rhine is the principal artery of capitalism in
Europe, so the Mekong brings wealth to all Indo-China.
The French sited their industries round Hanoi, where there
were coal-fields, but nevertheless the Mekong Delta remained
the richest part of the colony thanks to its great export of
rice, meat and vegetables. In spite of its wealth the Delta
region was also rebellious, since much of the peasants' earnings were taken by the plantation companies, the private
landlords, the church and above all the Chinese rice millers and
merchants, who also acted as usurers. When the revolutionary
socialists started up in the Twenties and Thirties, the largest
faction, the Trotskyists, put their faith in the Saigon proleta-
riat—refusing to recognize that it did not exist—while the
Russian-line Communists, the ancestors of the Viet Cong,
founded cells in the Delta villages, where they remain strong
today. Only a crude materialist of the Lassale school (*Man ist
was er isst*—Man is what he eats) could say that the Vietnam
war was about rice and only rice; nor is it easy to argue that
the United States intervened in Vietnam for the benefit of the
Wall Street capitalists, many of whom lost money because of
the war. It is true that the war made profit for the construction
firms, the makers of aircraft, guns, munitions and electronic
equipment. But this wealth derived from the United States
itself; almost nothing was taken out of Vietnam and countless
billions of dollars were poured in. The Vietnamese learned the
ethics of capitalism—the greed, the competitiveness, the love
of technological gadgets like cars, cameras and TV—but they
never acquired the capital by which this ethic is nourished.
The departure of the Americans and their money has left South

Vietnam actually poorer than before and has caused economic hardship, particularly over rice, that is helping the cause of the Communists. The Mekong maidens are amply revenged for the avarice of mankind.

When I first went to Can Tho in the Sixties I was both amused and depressed by the US economic advisers, who wanted to make this region 'the goddam richest region in Asia'. They jabbered of duck farms, giant melons, crash programs for pumpkins, irrigation systems, tractor loans, aerial crop-spraying and, always, 'miracle rice'.* 'I want to see the day', one adviser informed me, 'when every peasant is saving up for a second Honda. I want to make this a real, get-up-and-go, greedy society.' And for a few years in the Sixties there really was some prosperity in the Delta. I talked to peasants with only a few hectares of land who admitted to earning thousands of dollars a year from ducks (the feathers earn more than the meat and the eggs), from growing pumpkins, tomatoes, melons and of course rice, now harvested twice a year thanks to the new American methods. Many peasants possessed at least one motorcycle as well as an outboard motor for river travel. The village elders of Xuan Dong said with sincerity that the Americans had helped them to grow richer, but of course such prosperity was found only in regions that were 'secure' and therefore immune from bombing, artillery strikes and combat—although not immune to pillage by ARVIN. In the less secure ports of the Delta, hundreds of thousands of villagers fled to Saigon and the other towns, leaving their land to waste.

Even in Saigon during the Sixties, the lack of productive industries was in part concealed by the false boom of America's war economy. The construction companies spent more than a million dollars a day on roads, airports, barracks and houses,

* Last year I suggested, jokingly, to an American adviser that they ought to introduce a strain of 'miracle opium' to bolster the economy. The joke flopped.

electrical installations and harbours. More thousands of Vietnamese were employed on the communications network, now run by a subsidiary of ITT. There were hundreds of thousands of jobs for clerks, secretaries, interpreters, mess orderlies, laundresses, drivers and mechanics. On the fringe of America's war economy there were black marketeers, pedlars of stolen goods and equipment, bar girls, prostitutes and pimps. Perhaps two or three million Vietnamese were directly or indirectly employed in the service of 600,000 Americans. Yet almost none of the goods and equipment used in the US war effort were actually manufactured or grown in Vietnam. Everything from the planes, tanks and ammunition down to the tinned turkey, soft drinks and cigarettes were imported, largely from the United States. When these duty-free goods were sold on the black market they undercut goods from the local factories which produce, for example, beer, cigarettes, cement, clothing and barbed wire, so that after the war South Vietnam's industry had been actually weakened. Much of the wealth gained by the war profiteers was turned into gold or dollars and salted away in Swiss banks or invested in foreign property; virtually none was re-invested in Vietnam. It was the Japanese, not local capitalists, who got the benefit of the brief boom in luxury consumer goods such as TV and radio sets, air-conditioners, tape-recorders and motor scooters. The Honda company alone sold 200,000 vehicles, most of them to Saigon itself, which enjoyed what journalists called a 'Honda society' or a 'Honda revolution'. In the early days of this boom I remember seeing an Australian stare at a schoolgirl on a scooter before exclaiming: 'I never thought I'd live to see Asian sheilas mechanised'. The scooter and the motor car had become emblems of pride to the Saigon bourgeoisie but emblems of hate to poorer people, whose public transport had been removed and who did not dare bicycle through the murderous traffic. Just as the heroin rings made addicts of the country's youth, so foreign salesmen 'pushed' and then got people 'hooked' on private transport, driven by petrol, the very life-blood of capitalism.

As late as the Seventies there were still Americans who declared that when peace came, South Vietnam was 'ready for economic take-off'. A peace agreement was signed early in 1973 but there has been no sign of the take-off. The American withdrawal meant that about 300,000 Vietnamese lost their jobs in a few days, followed by gradual dismissals later in the year. Both the United States and Japan cut down government aid, which was in no way replaced by private investment. In vain the Saigon government painted the charm of the country to foreign capitalists: a population large enough to provide a local market; an educated and well trained labour force; timid trade unions and an average pay rate one-sixth that of neighbouring Singapore; tax holidays for investors and permission to take out or remit 100 per cent of the profits. These advantages could not compensate for the political uncertainty which worried investors more with every breach of the peace treaty.

As the cost of living rose by about 5 per cent a month, so earnings fell, causing poverty and starvation. A Saigon car dealer reported in August 1973 that sales were coming at one a month, compared to 100 a month in August the previous year. Professional and executive men who had earned 100,000 P a month when working for the Americans were reduced to jobs at only a tenth of that salary. One morning I looked from my hotel in Saigon at a huge crowd of young women assembled outside the offices of the National TV company of Japan, which had made so much profit during the boom. Each month this company interviewed 400 applicants for about 20 jobs, paying 7,000 P (about £5) a month. Most of these applicants had held clerical jobs with the Americans at about 15,000 P, when the piastre had double the purchasing power.

The Vietnamese can accept the loss of luxuries like TV, Hondas, cigarettes and sweets, but they can barely stand the swift and amazing increase in the price of rice, which doubled in 1973. Rice is not only their staple diet but almost part of their civilisation, a food with ritual and magic importance. The very word rice is the same as that for food. By late 1973 the cost of rice was an inescapable part of any conversation, quite replacing the other question of when the fighting would stop. The magnitude of the problem was explained to me in stark terms by a hotel porter: 'I have a salary of 8,000 P a month. The rice I need for my wife and eight children costs 20,000 P.' To get even a half ration of rice, poor Vietnamese have had to stop buying clothes, medicine, meat, fish or vegetables, other than seasoning such as pimento. The Vietnamese newspapers carry dozens of stories of heads of families who have killed themselves because they could no longer provide. Many more turned to banditry, housebreaking or murder to get the money for rice.

It has often been said by people who should know better that South Vietnam was a poor, peace-loving country; it used to be, on the contrary, a rich, war-loving country, which is why the people are now so shocked by their present condition of beggary. Even now South Vietnam has not been reduced to the state of poverty normal in countries like India, or even to that of Europe after the Second World War. But the memory of their former wealth, or at least of full bellies, has encouraged the Vietnamese to demand why the rice-bowl of Asia is empty. With good reason, they put much of the blame on the greed or incompetence of the Thieu government.

The politics of rice cannot be understood without some outline of its economy, which itself is far from simple. In French times the paddy, or unthreshed rice, was sold by the peasants almost exclusively to Chinese merchants, who milled it at towns like My Tho and Can Tho before transporting it to Saigon. These merchants also acted as bankers or usurers, lending money to peasants during the wet summer season on the security of the paddy that is harvested at the end of the year. Since many peasants also paid part of their rice earnings as rent to their landlords, their work was unhappy and was to become even more so with independence. First the Diem regime and later the local military satraps took illegal cuts in money or rice both from the peasants and from the Chinese merchants, who passed on the cost to the consumer in increased prices. The consequent inflation delighted the merchants, who make loans to the peasants in payment for rice several months in advance, at current rates. Since the price of paddy always goes up, these Chinese have the unique luck to be gambling on a futures market in which there is no risk. They make perhaps 15 per cent on the purchase and 20 per cent on the loans, of which about half probably goes on bribes to the military.

The squeeze on the peasants, almost as much as the fighting, reduced the production of rice so that South Vietnam, once a major exporter, had to import ten per cent of its needs with American funds, from American rice fields. Even when they left early in 1973 the Americans kept on this subsidy but with the hopeful assumption that South Vietnam would soon grow self-supporting in rice. Logically the ceasefire should have meant that refugees in the towns returned to work the paddy fields; that the peasants would no longer be taxed on their crop by the troops of both sides and that therefore production of rice would go up and the price down. Why then did the price of rice not only increase but increase at twice the rate of other commodities, even including imported goods? One minor factor was the introduction of Value Added Tax which caused even more nuisance here than it did in Britain, since few of the smaller shops kept written accounts. However the VAT was soon amended, and since rice was affected less than other goods one must look elsewhere for the cause of the rice problem.

The Saigon press, egged on by the government, attempted to blame the Communists for the rice problem. They accused the

Provisional Revolutionary Government (PRG) of buying up rice (presumably with outside funds) and then selling it cheap for a propaganda effect. It was whispered around town that people who got into PRG territory could buy rice at 50P a kilo compared to the 200 P then current in Saigon. One must doubt that this traffic existed in any significant quantity since its cost to the PRG would have been stupendous; but it was much discussed in Saigon, with results quite different from those wished by the newspapers. Far from blaming the Communists for the price of rice in Saigon, people admired them for keeping the price down in PRG territory. But Thieu, or whoever launched this particular story, may have had other motives than propaganda at home. He may have wanted to frighten America into giving more aid; he may have wanted further excuses to break his side of the peace agreement; he may have been trying, by linking rice with the Communists, to get the rice trade into the army's hands.

As we have seen, Thieu used to finance his apparatus of power very largely out of the profit from the drug trade. This was lucrative when the heroin could be sold either to GI's or as illegal exports, paid for in dollars, but it was far less lucrative when the buyers were Vietnamese. Moreover, it must have occurred even to Thieu that he could not go on fighting the Communists if the young men of the country, its future soldiers, were physically ruined by heroin. During 1973, one must assume, Thieu looked around for other sources of revenue to feed his apparatus, and rice was the obvious answer. Although the province and district chiefs in the Delta got their share of the graft on rice, the largest share went to the merchants, three-quarters of whom were still Chinese. A plan was produced by which much of the rice was to be sold to a state purchasing agency (GSA) which, although nominally autonomous, would depend on the military government for the purchase and sale of rice. So in the summer of 1973 the GSA and the Chinese merchants were buying in rivalry from the peasants, the GSA at a fixed rate and the merchants on a free market. But powerful men in the Army, and in particular General Nguyen Vinh Nghi, commander of IV Corps at Can Tho, wanted complete state control of the rice trade and the exclusion of private merchants. General Nghi, who was described to me by one diplomat as 'simply a pirate', was not acting on socialist or *dirigiste* principles. He wanted a bigger share of the graft. He and Thieu found a surprising supporter in the American chief rice adviser (who shall be nameless) at the US Embassy in Saigon. This expert (let us call him 'Expert A') pronounced that Vietnam was acutely short of rice; that stocks in Saigon were low; that they must be built up by getting the peasants to sell to the GSA. This Expert A also supported the thesis that much of the missing rice had been sold to the Communists who then resold it cheap for propaganda.

Until visiting the Delta late in 1973, I had accepted the views put forward by Expert A, but while in the Delta I met another American rice expert, whom I must call 'Expert B', for I promised not to attribute his views by name. According to Expert B only a tiny amount of rice was going to the Communists, who, he said, were themselves going short. He said that far from there being a shortage in government territory, this was a bumper harvest; that 95 per cent of the quota was reaching Saigon; that far from stocks being low, there was a danger of a surplus, with some of the wet rice going to rot; that instead of hoarding rice, the government should immediately dump its stocks on the market to bring down the price and force the peasants to sell. At the end of this talk I asked Expert B what was the cause of the rice crisis, to which he replied: 'The American Embassy in Saigon.' He said that Expert A had been wrong throughout, that he would not admit his mistake and had accused Expert B of fudging statistics. 'We tell them there's plenty of rice going through to Saigon, and they turn round and tell us we're being fooled and the deliveries are being falsified. We say 95 per cent of the quota is going to

Saigon and they say it's only 50 or 60 per cent.' Back in Saigon I repeated these arguments to supporters of Expert A, who exclaimed in horror: 'Dump rice? If the price drops in Saigon, the peasants will sell illegally to the the VC or to Cambodia, where there's a terrible rice shortage.'

When experts fall out in so decisive a fashion, I feel permitted to give my own opinion: that there will always be a rice problem in South Vietnam until the wealth of the paddy fields belongs to the peasants who farm them and not to foreigners, landlords, merchants and military gangsters.

The damage done to South Vietnam by the imposition of capitalism was brought home by the fuel crisis in late 1973. The government that had suppressed public transport in the interest of the car and scooter trade, promised to bring back the Saigon buses in order to save fuel. The price of bicycles doubled, so that even people who managed to sell their Hondas still needed more money to buy the more primitive vehicle. A semi-humorous columnist in a Saigon newspaper quoted an English scientist to the effect that riding a bicycle made men sterile which would be popular in Saigon now that big families could not afford rice. At the height of the fuel crisis the Communists pulled off a master-stroke of psychological warfare by exploding the Shell oil storage tank at Nha Be and with it half the fuel reserves. For days the smoke made darkness at noon in Saigon, like a funeral pall for the death of the Honda Society.

In North Vietnam, I understand, there is no shortage either of fuel or of rice, while industry is recovering from the American bombing attacks. In contrast to Germany, it is the socialist part of this divided nation that has achieved more economic success. This may be in part due to the fact that North Vietnam and West Germany possessed a bigger industrial base, while South Vietnam and East Germany were more agricultural. Yet I believe that capitalism would not have flourished in North Vietnam, nor communism in West Germany. Even partisans of the two economic systems must concede that they are not equally suitable to every kind of society. Capitalism was more likely to succeed among the Germans, who were accustomed by centuries of tradition to the idea of private ownership in both industry and land. The Vietnamese, on the other hand, had remained a peasant people, with the ingrained idea that the land belonged to the village or clan. Commerce had always been the prerogative of the Chinese and later the French, so that the Vietnamese thought of capitalism as something foreign and therefore distasteful. Ambitious men entered the civil service or the professions, leaving money matters like property, investment and savings to their wives. Even the arch-anti-communist Ngo Dinh Diem tried to keep foreign capitalists out of South Vietnam, which was certainly one of the reasons for the American dislike of him. The present military leaders like Thieu and Ky have amassed considerable fortunes from drugs, graft and the sale of office but they are not really businessmen so much as warlords or uniformed gangsters. Their land and house purchases, their banking arrangements in Zurich and Hong Kong, and even much of the haggling over contracts and bribes are left to the elegant Madame Ky and to Madame Thieu, the First Lady.

Those Americans in Can Tho who once wanted to make the Mekong Delta a 'get-up-and-go, greedy society' have never returned to see the result of their labours. Certainly greed, or at least hunger, stares from the eyes of scores of tattered, whining beggars, many of them with missing limbs and all of them thin and sick. Rice, in the heart of the rice country, costs almost as much as in Saigon to those who do not live on their own farms. Some of the Chinese are fat but there are few fat Vietnamese under the rank of major, a fact I have established from careful observation. I cannot record as fact but as a definite impression the overwhelming nastiness of Can Tho: the filth, stench, waste, ugliness and the misery of the faces. It is a town where you start each morning in certainty that not one single enjoyable thing will happen during the day. After one horrible afternoon I locked myself in my hotel bedroom and tried to read but dropped off to sleep with the light on. I woke from a nightmare to find that the hag who collected the laundry had brought in a girl whom she was forcibly pressing upon me, the girl's body on mine and the girl's mouth (with ulcerous gums) on my mouth. After explaining that I was not in the mood, I went for a much-needed drink to a riverside café, remarkable for the fact that its staff occasionally smiled. There was a very loud tape of rock music from the United States, which I had heard the night before but could bear again. After some twenty minutes a commotion took place with the arrival of a young woman and two soldiers. All three were drugged and the girl promptly fell into unconsciousness. A legless beggar pushed himself to their table and started to tug at the trouser leg of one of the soldiers, who shouted a bit and stared round the café. The manager of the café told them to go, and then turning to me, whispered 'Heroin'. As this was going on, the tape started to play the rock version of Beethoven's finale to the Choral Symphony, with words roughly adapted from Schiller. While the two men staggered out of the café, holding their woman friend by the arms and legs, still followed by the legless beggar, the music rose into the blood-stirring, magnificent theme which was Beethoven's message of joy to all mankind.

Part Five
LAOS AND CAMBODIA

Some twenty years ago I made a long train journey with nothing to read except *Newsweek* (or maybe *Time*) containing a special report on Indo-China. I read it several times and by the end of the journey I knew which of the countries were Vietnam, Cambodia and Laos. I did not try to remember the names of the various politicians and kings but something about the countries stuck in my memory. I knew from then on that Vietnam was the serious place where communists were defying the French, while Laos and Cambodia were romantic countries of bells, gongs, gilt barges, bonzes, elephants and royal intrigue. The impression I gained was valid, for Vietnam really is distinct from the other two countries in Indo-China, whose very name implies the distinction. The Vietnamese were once ruled by the Chinese and share their respect for hard work, reason, education, good manners and discipline, tempered by tolerance. The Cambodians are a darker people with more of the Indian in their ethnic make-up as well as their character and religion. While Buddhism in Vietnam is superficial and streaked with animist heresies, in Cambodia it is pure and strong. Processions, ritual, magic and dance are just as important in politics as in the pagoda. The Laotians, although similar to the Thais by race, are just as good Buddhists as the Cambodians. Neither they nor the tribespeople who live in the mountains feel any affinity with the Vietnamese to the east. There was actual hostility in colonial times, for the French employed Vietnamese as clerks and officials in Laos and Cambodia, where they were joined by relatives who became

135

artisans and shopkeepers. However the resentment against the Vietnamese was never as fierce in Laos or Cambodia as it was in other countries where the colonial power used one subject people to govern another less advanced. The Vietnamese were never as unpopular as the Asians in East Africa or the Ibos in Northern Nigeria.

Because of their different history and tradition, the Laotians and Cambodians did not join the Vietnamese in the war against colonialism, although they accepted independence when it was offered them. When Vietnam was divided and the Communists in the south started their revolutionary struggle, there was no corresponding movement in the countries to the west. But as the fighting in Vietnam grew more intense, so Laos and then Cambodia were drawn into the struggle. The mountains of northern Laos, which are inhabited by tribes-people such as the Meos, had long suffered confused warfare. During the Second World War this area had been contested by the Nationalist Chinese, the Japanese and by French agents dropped in to train guerilla bands. During the subsequent war between the Vietnamese Communists and the French, the same people were propagandised and trained by both sides. When Laos became independent, the Nationalists and the Communists split between themselves under the leadership of two princely half-brothers, Souvanna Phouma and Souvanna-vong. Although Laos was divided both physically and politically, the division had none of the acrimony of the war in Vietnam. The number of troops committed was small; the battles reported had often not taken place; and both sides in 1962 joined in a tripartite coalition with yet another, right-wing group. They had been at war, but a war often akin to comedy.

In Cambodia until 1970 there was no war at all, thanks to the statesmanship of Prince Norodom Sihanouk, who governed the country first as King, then after his abdication, as Prime Minister. As King, in colonial times, Sihanouk characteristically took both sides in turn in the war of the French against the Vietnamese Communists. With independence in 1954, he just as characteristically made allies of both the French and the Vietnamese Communists against his enemies, who included the South Vietnamese, the Thais, the Chinese Communists and the Americans. In parts of Cambodia there were skirmishes between Sihanouk troops and his right-wing enemies, certain river pirates and the Khmer Rouges, a small communist group, but the country remained the most peaceful in South-east Asia.

By 1973, the year of the ceasefire agreement, Cambodia and Laos were not involved in the war but were suffering from it more than Vietnam itself. In both countries at least a third of the population were homeless refugees from the American B-52 raids. In both countries communist troops led by Vietnamese had won much popular support in the countryside. This spreading of war and communism to all Indo-China must be blamed on the very country, America, that had tried to prevent it. By trying to stamp out the fire in Vietnam she had raised sparks to ignite the rest of the forest.

Cambodia 1963

I first went to Cambodia in November 1963, on the way back to London after a tour of Japan. I had wanted to go to South Vietnam, but this was just after the murder of Diem, and the Consulate in Hong Kong was not giving visas to journalists. (Next time it was the Cambodians who would not give me a visa, and then the Vietnamese again after I wrote things they did not like. The Laos never refuse a visa, although I was once delayed when their Saigon consulate ran out of ink for the visa stamp.) From my first day in Cambodia I thought it the most wonderful place in the world but since I was new to the tropics I had nothing to compare it with. Since then I have been to many places in the tropics and I still think that Cam-

bodia was the best. I wrote an article at the time advising
people to go there soon as such a delightful place could not
remain delightful; nor has it.

I remember Phnom Penh as a city of broad streets, trees,
flowers and flamboyants; serene and smiling people; of dusk
at a café beside the river and after dark the floating dance halls
where Vietnamese girls, insubstantial as shadows, swayed in
the moonlight to music that I had never before heard or
imagined. In the mornings I sat under the green awning at
La Paillotte in the market place, drinking orange juice and
bitter tea, watching the slow crowds by the foodstalls crammed
with the abundance of a fertile land. There were Vietnamese
lunches and French dinners and late at night a soft tap on the
door from a barefoot girl who smiled as you unwound her
from her sarong.

After a few days in Phnom Penh I took a Chinese bus to
Siem Reap, near the temples of Angkor, the most famous
monument of the East. I remember the first sight of paddy
fields in which water buffaloes grazed, almost every one with
a white egret perched on its back picking at insects; of vegeta-
tion so bright and green that it hurt the eyes; of waits at ferries
beside broad rivers the colour of milk chocolate; of gaudy
pagodas and wooden houses on stilts, surrounded by dogs and
ducks; of the steaming atmosphere, the ripe smells and the
water everywhere, giving a sense of fecundity, of nature spawn-
ing, flowering, ripening and on heat. Cambodia is so fertile
that only a war or grotesque mismanagement can produce real
hunger or poverty. The river Tonle Sap, which waters the
central rice fields, has the odd habit of changing direction.
During the dry season it flows north to south into the Mekong
but during the wet season the Mekong flood pushes water
upstream, creating a big lake. The lucky peasants get two
floods for their rice paddies and two runs of fish for their
nets. They say that Cambodians fish for elephants and hunt
for fish, because when the Tonle Sap suddenly drops, the

elephants get stuck in the mud and the fish get stuck in the branches of trees.

In this countryside, even more than Phnom Penh, I got the romance of the East as I knew it from Conrad and Kipling and as I imagined it still existed in other countries apart from Cambodia, although probably even in those days the old East existed only in Laos, Cambodia, Burma and parts of Indonesia. This was the East of Conrad's *Youth*, of Kipling's *Road to Mandalay*. 'A neater, sweeter maiden in a cleaner, greener land'; well, it may be banal but it is also true. And in 1963 one could still visit Angkor, the strangest though not the most beautiful architectural work in the world. It is a city of temples spread out over an area about the size of Manchester but many of them concealed or even smothered by jungle. The largest and most important temples like Angkor Wat and the Bayon—with its forty leering Buddhas—have been tidied, cleaned and made ready for inspection but it was also fun to wander in search of smaller ruins, or even smaller stones. It was my first time in a jungle (they are rare in South-east Asia) and I was awed by the rank stench and the hubbub of screeches, purrs, twangling and yelps—like a dog that has been hit by a motor car. Once turning a corner I came on a troupe of monkeys and once on a TV actress from New York, but nobody could complain that Angkor was spoiled by tourists. The jungle was too powerful to be tamed; the temples too fearsome to be vulgarised.

For Angkor is rather a frightening place. It was built in the 12th century by one of the last Khmer rulers before the empire was crushed by Siam. Only a megalomaniac, like a Pharaoh or Stalin, would have started a project on so huge a scale with so little variety of invention. For beautiful though they may be, the temples at Angkor and even the statues and friezes are endlessly repetitious in concept and detail. The mind becomes dulled by the hundredth identical Buddha, with lips set in unchanging smile, by the dancing girls with their arms ever akimbo so that you cease to believe that they ever danced.

There is none of the life or rhythm of Greek sculpture and architecture. This deathly, static quality affected the film of Conrad's *Lord Jim* which was shot on location at Angkor a few weeks after my visit. They had already planted a few Royal Palms 'to give atmosphere' to the site, but in vain, for Angkor already had atmosphere but it was not the atmosphere of a Borneo fishing village.

The choice of location was not the only trouble facing this film company, because Prince Sihanouk at the time was in one of his xenophobic fits; indeed quite by accident I had arrived in a time of historic importance. Since becoming king at the age of 18 in 1941, Sihanouk had made numerous shifts of policy, most striking of which was his abdication in 1955 to go into active politics. Thanks to his strong personality and the great prestige of the monarchy he appeared unchallengeable in domestic politics, but he felt threatened by countries abroad. The Thais, Cambodia's ancient enemy, had taken much of the country during the Second World War, and had broken diplomatic relations, as had South Vietnam, which sheltered a number of Sihanouk's enemies. The crisis in late 1963 was said to have been ignited by Sihanouk's listening to a broadcast from Saigon, in which an opponent made lewd and untrue assertions about his sex life. The enraged Prince himself went on the air for hours on end screaming abuse at these enemies in his piercing falsetto; I wrote in my diary at the time that he sounded less like a head of state making a diplomatic détente than a schoolgirl hockey player accusing another of 'sticks' in a vital match. In his fury against the Saigon government for the shelter it gave to his slanderers, Sihanouk came out in support of the Viet Cong. Afterwards he went on to attack the Americans, who were advising Saigon, and therefore enemies by association. In a series of noisy pronouncements he nationalised trade and banking, asked for economic aid from Communist China, refused American aid and finally shut down their embassy.

I applied for an interview, and by way of reply found a front-page lead story in next day's *Dépêches de Cambodge* denouncing those journalists who thought they could see Prince Sihanouk without having applied months in advance. The same issue carried a long attack not just on the Americans but, rather ominously, on 'the Anglo-Saxons ... who have put about the rumour of a mad Sihanouk'. And indeed such rumours were going about. I was told at the American Embassy that nothing could keep Cambodia from instant and total bankruptcy; that all foreign investment would be withdrawn; that the Red Chinese would soon be in charge of the army and the police; and that Sihanouk was off his onion. I much regret that I in part believed them and wrote an article (thankfully unsigned) predicting trouble ahead; for this I was roundly but rightly attacked by Peter Duval Smith, who knew that part of the world very much better than I did.

Cambodia 1968

When I next went to Cambodia in May 1968, I saw it with some knowledge of what was happening in the rest of Indo-China. Clean, graceful Phnom Penh now seemed more than a world away from Saigon or the greedy, concrete squalor of Bangkok. Moreover, I saw with delight that contrary to the predictions of five years back, Cambodia was not merely peaceful but prosperous. There were excellent new roads, railways, a deep-water port and hospitals. The 500 primary schools and 200 high schools had a yielded a literacy rate of 90 per cent. The economy, without US aid or advice, had survived every prophecy of disaster. Rubber, tea and rice were produced as before. The French and Chinese businessmen had increased their investment. Indeed in the first three years after the expulsion of the Americans there had been record balance-of-payments surpluses. In 1966 the Prince had relaxed his programme of austerity and allowed too much to be spent on luxury imports; but still the budget was balanced, nobody quite understood how. Statistics reported a drop in the rice sold to the state purchasing boards, and some of the rice experts thought that production was dropping. In fact the peasants were getting a better price by selling their crop to the Viet Cong, who used Cambodia as a supply base. Since the VC paid with US dollars—bought on the black market in Saigon—the Cambodian government got a bonus of hard-currency earnings.

Cambodia still took foreign aid in the form of teachers from France, one or two factories from China and experts from East Europe, but it was clear that her greatest gains had been negative. She had escaped the harmful effects of American aid, namely a huge over-equipped army more interested in politics than in war; a class of US officials whose high and ostentatious standard of living provoked envy and hatred; and a second bureaucracy of corrupt local officials using US jargon and Swiss bank accounts.

In foreign affairs Sihanouk maintained his 'bad neighbour' policy towards Thailand and South Vietnam. Referring to the border with Laos, he said in May that year: 'We shall not surrender so much as a tree or an ant that bites us, provided that ant is Cambodian.' Nor had he allowed the Communists to get undue influence in his country. When the Chinese Embassy tried to send Red Guards through Phnom Penh they were threatened with instant expulsion. The police arrested, imprisoned and sometimes expelled many Communist agitators, sometimes making personal searches in Phnom Penh of everybody of Chinese or Vietnamese appearance. The Prince remained friendly with North Vietnam but continued to rail at the 'Maoists'.

However the favourite enemy was the United States. As the Pentagon papers later revealed, the United States had begun illegal and secret air strikes on Cambodia but at this time denied any violations of territory. A grisly monument had been set up by the river in Phnom Penh built of a wrecked US plane and bits of a helicopter and armoured cars claimed to have been destroyed on Cambodian territory. The Americans said that the plane had been shot down by the VC over South Vietnam and was already crashing across the border when Cambodian troops gave it a final burst of machine-gun fire, afterwards bagging another man's pheasant. But no doubt surrounded the capture of the beer ship. This unfortunate vessel, crewed by Filipinos but guarded by two American soldiers, was sailing from Vung Tau on the coast of South Vietnam, bound for Can Tho in the Mekong Delta. The skipper took two wrong turns, lost his way and sailed up the wrong stream into Cambodia. Prince Sihanouk at first wanted to ransom the two soldiers for two US bulldozers, but later relented and freed them, keeping the beer.

The quirks and about-turns of Cambodian foreign affairs reflected the man who took all decisions in public life. He was looked upon by most foreigners either with rage or derision but this year I came to realise just how effective he was. Critics complained, I admit with some justification, that he busied himself too much in the ordinary life of the country. In Cambodia's film industry he was the top director, producer, scriptwriter, cameraman and star. A composer and saxophonist, he frequently went to the microphone at diplomatic receptions to play a few numbers in a relaxed Las Vegas style. A poster of him in football shorts said he was 'father of the country's sport', although he is better at horsemanship than at football. He loved to be photographed planting rice with the peasants or hurling gifts of cloth to them from his helicopter. He relished state visits from foreign dignitaries (especially women, like Jackie Kennedy and Princess Margaret), parties, religious feasts and any ceremony that required his gifts as a showman. He laughed a great deal, made shrill speeches, fussed over the guests and flattered the ladies. The monthly magazine *Kambudja* (editor: Prince Norodom Sihanouk) used to give much space to these state occasions, printing scores of photographs of the head of state.

A prolific journalist in his own right, the Prince was quick to refuse those foreign colleagues who wrote rude things of Cambodia, in particular those who called it 'small' or still worse 'tiny'. He once published a list of all the countries in the world ranked by population and size, proving that 'tiny' Cambodia was far from the end of the list. He believed with good reason that most foreign journalists were unfair to his country and filed their names under 'friendly', 'unfriendly' or 'uncertain'.* The Prince may have distrusted most foreign powers but he was always ready to learn from them and to adapt what was useful for his country. France has given her language, which the Cambodians speak very well (much better than do the Vietnamese), her sense of style and her *bonne cuisine*, which the Prince enjoyed so much that he had to keep going for cures. During these visits to Grasse or Vichy, the Phnom Penh newspapers would carry respectful news items such as: 'This week Prince Norodom Sihanouk lost 10 kilos.' In 1968 he had lost several kilos but unfortunately regained them when, in a series of visits to French schools, he first made a speech then took the pupils out for a feast at a local pastry shop—matching them cake for cake.

The Prince disapproved of China, but during a state visit there he was much impressed by the absence of night clubs. On his return to Phnom Penh he proclaimed that dance halls were nationalised—and was furious when an American magazine said that his mother had taken over the brothel trade. The Prince even borrowed one British idea. In October 1966 he had ordered a general election, only to find that too many 'wrong' candidates were elected with views well to the right of himself. As head of state he could have simply dismissed the new

---

* I wrote after this visit: 'Even if no-one in England bothers to finish this article, I can count on one reader in Phnom Penh'. Prince Sihanouk took the joke and wrote a pleasant letter to the newspaper.

government and installed himself as the Premier, but he sagely resisted this overbearing measure and instead announced that the country was going to have a 'Loyal Opposition'. The Opposition was formed and started to publish a daily *Bulletin of the Counter-Government*, under the editorship of, but you guessed, Prince Norodom Sihanouk. Savage articles from his pen accused the government of graft, sloth and incompetence until the Prime Minister became so upset that he resigned and was replaced—by Prince Norodom Sihanouk. However the new Prime Minister continued to edit the *Bulletin of the Counter-Government*, although that journal grew markedly less critical in its tone.

Those aspects of Cambodian life that foreigners found strange, or even absurd, were nevertheless true to the country's tradition and culture. Buddha himself taught that the truth, the Middle Way, was sometimes arrived at through paradox and confusion. Prince Sihanouk ruled in the same style as the ancient emperors during the European Dark Ages. They too had been cultural mentors, priests of the state religion, philosophers of the national will and masters of public ceremony. Modern Cambodia had an unbroken heritage from the old Khmer Empire, with customs, religion and monarchy little changed. The same could not be said of neighbouring Thailand which wanted breakneck modernisation with instant aggressive capitalism. Cambodia under Sihanouk preferred merely to taste new ideas, selecting those which were suitable to her culture but casting out those that were merely flashy or harmful. Bangkok University had acquired a Faculty of Public Relations and Mass Communications but millions of Thai peasants were, and still are, illiterate. Cambodia had rejected sociological cant and American jargon, yet its schools were excellent.

Sihanouk was often attacked because Cambodia would not admit 'hippies' or 'travelling people', the long-haired, gentle and rather gormless youngsters who roam the East. An article in the *Bulletin of the Counter-Government* set out to explain this apparently harsh attitude. The writer first explained that Cambodians sympathised with the hippy dislike of modern western society. They too were in revolt against industrialism and violence and hypocrisy; they wanted to go back to Rousseau's ideal of the Natural Man; so far so good. But in Cambodia, the article went on, 'the advance of science has not yet destroyed the foundation of our culture, which remains firm. The visiting hippies would have more to learn from us than to teach us. And in order to learn they should modify their behaviour out of respect for our culture and thought.'

I ended my own article on Cambodia with words that now read sadly: 'The Chinese, if they wanted to, could take over Cambodia in a week. So possibly could the Americans, the Thais and either Vietnam. It would not matter much in the balance of world power. Yet for anyone who has been to Cambodia its loss would be a disaster. Of course it is rather corrupt and monarchical, and a little authoritarian. It is a country for escapists from things like the Cult of Violence, student power, the space race, sociological surveys, debates on the Permissive Society, Mao's Thoughts, *Time* magazine (which is banned), the "white heat of technology", traffic and war. "I have seen the future—and it works!" said one journalist after visiting Lenin's Russia. Well I have seen the past—and it works!'

Cambodia 1970

When I next went to Cambodia it was only three months after Sihanouk's fall but already his followers occupied half the country and surrounded Phnom Penh. An attack on the city was imminent, said the newspaper I read on the plane; it has stayed imminent since. There was no sign of the war in Phnom Penh itself but plentiful signs of the political changes wrought by Sihanouk's overthrow. I was surprised and depressed by the speed of the Americans in moving in as military advisers, intelligence agents, liaison officers with the Lon Nol administration and apologists on its behalf. Within twenty minutes I started to talk with a thin man in white shirt and black tie (almost the CIA uniform in this region) who was distributing carbines and drove a car with an 007 licence plate (he did not think this funny). In my hotel there was a great deal of hobnobbing between two crew-cut Americans of military appearance and two Soviet 'journalists', who shunned the rest of the press corps. The Soviet Union was one of the first countries to rat on Sihanouk after his fall and one of the first to rat on Lon Nol when he in turn seemed to be losing three years later.

It was depressing to hear foreigners—the businessmen, diplomats and journalists—discuss the reasons for Sihanouk's fall and why they considered it salutary. He had been too domineering. People had been afraid of him. University graduates had been made to teach in the provinces instead of living in Phnom Penh. These were the arguments of the Phnom Penh bourgeoisie, the people who spoke English or French and could get the ear of foreigners. I argued back that this was a counter-revolution designed to create the kind of military gangster capitalism found in countries like Thailand, Taiwan, South Vietnam, South Korea and the Philippines; that Sihanouk was still popular with the peasants. The stock reply to this argument was that Sihanouk's government had not managed to cure the endemic dysentery which had given Cambodia such a high infant mortality rate. These old arguments do not matter now but even in retrospect I am shocked by the way that westerners used to explain and even condone the pogrom of Vietnamese by the Lon Nol government.

During the first few weeks after the coup, Cambodian troops were permitted or even ordered to kill some hundreds of Vietnamese, most of them fishermen on the Tonle Sap. The corpses were thrown into the river and floated downstream, some of them getting as far as Vietnam, where they were photographed and shown in the press. In an attempt to stir up anti-Vietnamese hatred, the Lon Nol government staged a kind of pageant in the football stadium at which Khmer troops were shown murdering ugly foreigners, while monster Vietnamese conical hats were soaked in petrol and set alight. I saw similar shows on Cambodian TV. It is not unusual for right-wing revolutionaries to try to win public support by exploiting xenophobia: Hitler used it against the Jews, General Amin against the Asians and the military junta in Chile against foreign left-wing refugees. But this is a short-sighted way of gaining support, even when it exploits real public hostility, as Hitler did in Germany. The pogrom by Lon Nol was triply foolish because it alienated the Vietnamese and drove them into the Communists' ranks; it alienated the government of Saigon on which he depended for military help; and it alienated most Cambodians, who have been living quite peaceably with the Vietnamese over the centuries. Although many Cambodians resented the Vietnamese merchants and shopkeepers, few wanted to get rid of Vietnamese peasants and fishermen and certainly not by a massacre. I have never heard a Cambodian try to excuse the massacre or even speak of it without some kind of apology. Yet I have heard the killings explained and by implication justified by western diplomats and journalists. And paradoxically, these were just the kind of liberal-minded people who would condemn ill-treatment of Asians and blacks in Britain or the United States, where such minority groups are objects of far more dislike than the Vietnamese in Cambodia. Perhaps in the tender conscience of western, white liberals, it is racialist to accuse another race of being illiberal to a third.*

* I noticed the same thing in Uganda during the expulsion of the Asians. The British newspapers were full of stories of how these people were hated by the Africans, yet the Africans themselves expressed only the mildest ill-feelings. The wretched Asians were kicked out of a country where they had lived for years and were accepted to go to a country, Britain, where there is strong and widespread dislike of them.

What depressed me most in Cambodia was the sight of the combat reporters and photographers who had come in from Saigon to find a hotter story. Many of these were shrewd and respected men who liked Cambodia and were sorry to see it at war, but there were also the 'combat freaks', the young photographers who, from some mental disorder, enjoy danger, violence and the sight of wounds and death. The finest photographs of Vietnam were taken by Philip Jones Griffiths, who had been a conscientious objector to British military service and never ceased to be outraged by the cruelties of war. He took many ordinary action shots, but his best work stressed the political forces which started the war and will one day resolve it. One of the pictures in his collection *Vietnam Inc* shows a VC woman prisoner who had been shot in the spine and kept all day with her hands behind her back. When Griffiths reproached the officer, he replied: 'What's the use? When the GVN (government troops) have interrogated her, she'll only be raped and killed anyway.' Another photograph shows a VC prisoner who had fought for three days with a cooking bowl strapped to his stomach to keep his guts from spilling out. Griffiths was the only man to photograph the computer and its fatuous, smiling attendants that produced the Hamlet Evaluation System; he was the only man to show Vietnamese who had been driven out of their senses by war and now lay chained to their beds in a lunatic asylum; and he was the first to show Vietnamese boys injecting heroin into their arms. Pictures like those did not get into the western newspapers, which preferred to give readers vicarious thrills from combat. It was in part this failure by press and TV to show what the war was really about that explains why America lost it. And now the same thing was happening in Cambodia. In Vietnam the combat photographers commuted to war by helicopter. In Cambodia they could go by car from Phnom Penh as far as they dared up one of the highways—a lethal grandmother's footsteps, which many players lost.

Cambodia 1973

In December 1973, almost exactly ten years since I had first come to Cambodia, the one-time paradise had disappeared from the earth. Three years of American bombing had wiped out most of the villages, killed hundreds of thousands of people and driven two million refugees to beggary in Phnom Penh. The Communist and Sihanouk forces, both led by the North Vietnamese, controlled two-thirds of the country, including Angkor, and were camped by the suburbs of Phnom Penh. I stayed at the Poste Hotel by the river and each night was continually woken by small-arms fire from sentries shooting at clumps of weed. One night the noise increased in volume and went on for many minutes, but it was not till days later I heard that there had indeed been a commando raid by water. Phnom Penh was receiving mortar, rocket and terrorist bomb attacks; not many—but not many are needed to make a city unpleasant. As in Vietnam, it was the poor who suffered most from the war: no food in the orphanages, no drugs in the hospital and rice risen to ten times its previous price. Even some of the Phnom Penh bourgeoisie now regretted the Sihanouk days, so that the French word one must often heard was *avant*. '*Avant, monsieur, on mangeait bien. Avant, il-y-avait la paix*'. However the war has been profitable to the rascally generals and ministers who deal in sales of rice, drugs and arms, much of them sold to the other side. President Lon Nol is said with authority to have banked over $80m, so he was not much put out when his wife was apprehended at Paris airport with $140,000 hidden in two teddy bears.

The wretchedness of Cambodia is still partly relieved by the old charm which infects even the armed services. The commander-in-chief, Marshal Sostien Fernandes, is a Filipino former band-leader, once hired by Sihanouk to accompany his saxophone. He is a chirpy rogue, who much enjoys publicity and parades, but his timidity in attack has got him the nickname 'Fernandes Hideaway'. The army has been much troubled by astral events, particularly the eclipse of the sun, which the troops interpreted as a giant toad and attacked with millions of shots. When I was here they were expecting more wasted ammunition and even a coup d'etat if the Kohoutek meteor should be visible in Cambodia. The Cambodian air force provided some comedy when it bombed Phnom Penh airport by accident shortly before landing there. On two occasions air force pilots bombed the Presidential palace before flying to Communist territory. The first time the pilot missed by about half a mile. The second pilot scored a direct hit and flew off doing a victory roll, not having discovered beforehand that Lon Nol was out of town. I saw a sentry apparently aiming his carbine at the ministry he was guarding until, coming closer, I saw he was shooting at birds in a tree; I smiled at a pretty girl sentry who burst into giggles and ducked so that only the top of her rifle was visible over the sandbags.

It is said to be bad manners to write about English phrase-books for foreigners but an exception must be made for '1200 Khmer-English Phrases' by Som-Vicheth & San-Sarun, a work that was lent to me by my friend James Fenton. The actual English is fairly correct, or at least not laughably incorrect, and the unusualness of the book lies in the senti-ments expressed. It is almost a work of political significance for it shows the difficulties of communication faced by Ameri-cans in Cambodia. In fact Phrase 651 reads: 'I used to be employed by the American Embassy in Phnom Penh'. Here are some other phrases, selected almost at random, but in sequence.

> Don't make goo-goo eyes at me. She cast sheep's eyes at me. My eye! Go away, brazen-face! No one loves you. He died of love. He died for his Nation. Don't make faces at me! Don't purse your lips at me! Behold my bosom naked to you. No necking and crop allowed. He is a muff. This country is rife with foreign spies. Why rustle? For God's sake go away! My hair stands on end with

terror. Your book is the best seller. Your sneers and jeers are hard
to bear. You thickhead. I am thirstless of power. I used to travel
England from end to end. He is surnamed a hunter of girls.
What a swell you are! Bad boy you break wind very badly
(with too bad smell). She exclaimed 'I won't'. You are a bad hat.
Don't hiss at me! You are quite lousy (slang). Vagina (pussy).
War is a rude reminder. She is a poisonous snake. Unfasten your
clothes. Don't violate my virginity. This guy is a local dude. The
independence of the country is at stake. The fighting remains a
stalemate. Don't splash me.

Laos in the late Sixties

One former diplomat who had served twenty years in Indo-
China, much of the time in Laos, decided one day to write a
book of memoirs. He smoked a few pipes of opium and perhaps
swallowed a glass of whiskey then sat down at the typewriter,
only to find that he could not remember a thing. My acquain-
tance with Laos goes back only seven years and I cannot have
spent more than a few months there in total, but I find much
the same difficulty as the diplomat. For example I cannot
remember my first visit. I know that I went, in spring 1967, for
the entrance and exit stamps are there in my former passport,
and I know that I wrote a letter from there, which did not
arrive. In those days few letters or cables left the country. Nor
did I write any articles about my experiences, which must have
been too bizarre to be believable. Indeed I have only once been
in Laos when there was any news of a kind acceptable to a
newspaper, and that, very appropriately, was the last state
visit by Vice-President Spiro Agnew. I did not write about that
until some weeks afterwards, when I was back in London, for
the mood of Laos is not conducive to work, especially writing
newspaper articles. I have never kept up a diary there, and even
my pocket notebook on this last visit contained no entry
except an *aide memoire* as to which room I had taken in which
hotel. One can forget even such things in Vientiane. To tell
the truth, one can very quickly go rather to pieces. I must

therefore apologise if this chapter on Laos is rather short, vague and lacking in deep political insights. I have never made head nor tail of the place.

Only one journalist ever understood Laos and she was fired by her news agency because the true reports she filed were not as acceptable as the fiction filed by everyone else. How can one explain a country where three armies, Right, Left and Neutralist, are locked in vague battle over the misty plains; where the main industry, opium-growing, is backed by the CIA; where the capital can be shelled by its own police in an attack on the army (or maybe the other way round, I cannot remember); where the peace talks began over a fancy-dress party at which the US Ambassador was attired, if my memory is correct, as Sinbad the Sailor? Like the drunken porter in *Macbeth* or the gravedigger in *Hamlet*, Laos provided the comic relief in the Indo-China tragedy. Of course, it was not really funny, especially for the Laotians in the hinterland which was fought over and bombed for years as a result of America's effort to block the Ho Chi Minh Trail. Many of the hill tribes, like the Meos, were cut down, dispersed and forced into refugee camps where they had to wear labels denoting their tribal origin. How must it have felt to be labelled 'Ethnic Yao'? The legendary civilisation of temples and gongs was corroded by Americanism. At certain festivals, which consisted mostly of singing erotic songs, the papier-maché figures of copulating tortoises no longer appeared—thanks to the protests of the US Women's Association.

In spite of everything, Vientiane remained a delightful capital—I was going to say capital city, but capital village would be much more appropriate. I arrived there by plane from Saigon in May 1968 to find that I had lighted on the day of the Rocket Festival. It was the first plane out of Saigon after a week of the heavy fighting that I described in chapter two of this book. The day before I had had to fling myself on the tarmac of Le Loi street as a rocket went overhead and exploded in Nguyen Hue.

It was all the more pleasant therefore to come to a city of toy, ceremonial rockets, which are fired southwards across the Mekong into Thailand. The rockets of wood and paper are about forty feet in length and decorated with bright pictures of dragons, tigers and elephants. They make a pleasant swoosh on firing and there is quite a cheer from the crowd if the rocket gets anywhere near the far shore. Some of the soldiers had flowers stuck in the mesh of their helmets and everyone seemed to be walking hand in hand. I am told there is an even better festival when people throw buckets of water over each other, but I do not seem to have been in Laos when it was taking place. There is the story told of a Russian spy disguised as a *Pravda* correspondent who arrived in Vientiane on the day of this festival and received a bucketful of water over his serge suit. Enraged, he went to his hotel room, dried the suit in the sun and went out into the street to be drenched with water once more, thrown by the same man out of the same bucket.

That year, and in 1967 and 1969, I slowly took in the sights of Vientiane and the personalities of the time. In 1968—it must have been that year—I first stayed at the Constellation Hotel, whose Corsican Vietnamese proprietor M. Cavalleri is an important and likeable Laos businessman. It was the time of the student riots in Paris but I could not understand at first why he was so anxious to hear my guess about whether De Gaulle would fall and the franc be devalued. I kept answering no to both questions, which always seemed to re-assure him, and at last he took me into his office to show me why. The tables were stacked with francs and cheques he had bought at big discounts from local French and Laotians who feared a devaluation. His deals were watched with great interest by one of the guests at the Constellation, an American pilot who had retired here seven years earlier and also wanted to go into business. 'Don't you think Vientiane is an ideal place to found a stock exchange?' he would ask as we mumbled and turned away our eyes. There was an expatriate Englishman who used to swim fully dressed in the Mekong and then dry off in the sand before coming round for a beer to the hotel where he lectured me on his two favourite writers, Yeats and Hitler. Sophisticates claimed that they never went to the White Rose night club, of world-famous indecency, where the floor show of one girl is talked of with admiration even by her envious colleagues: 'She smoke ten cigarettes at once. She suck in like that. My pussy, she no can. Her pussy, she do.' However you generally meet someone you know in the White Rose, where I was once given a briefing by a distinguished British diplomat who had both hands under the knickers of two of the hostesses.

Although Laos was then at war it was still in theory at peace, under a treaty drawn up in 1962 and afterwards broken by the Americans. In theory the government still included Communist ministers, who did not take up their posts, but the Pathet Lao did keep up a compound, a kind of embassy. Their representative, Colonel Sot, was said to be quite a character so I paid him a visit to hear his usual speech, which always ended in Voltaire's phrase '*Il faut cultiver notre jardin*'. It was all the more strange since his garden had gone to seed and was almost jungle. The Pathet Lao compound was quite close to the US Embassy—and also an anti-embassy which had been set up by a radical Boston psychiatrist who ran Vientiane's first psychedelic night club. It had an exotic kaleidoscope which fascinated the small son of the Vietnamese lady with whom I was then familiar. He would sit watching this thing until curfew time while I was anxious to get back to the house in the industrial quarter of Vientiane. She called it the industrial quarter but I never found more than one factory, which produced rubber shoes and whose assembly belt seemed to be run by an outboard motor. Because of this lady I came back to Vientiane from working in Saigon and Bangkok, where she wanted me to obtain various contraband matter. She wanted dollars from Saigon (in return for gold) and from Bangkok she wanted precious stones and erotic literature. 'I have only one erotic book, she would wail at me, 'but it's by the Marquis de Sade and its too sadistic!'

Laos 1973

Early in 1973 I came up to Laos from Singapore, making part of the journey on the enjoyable railway. It was just after the ceasefire in South Vietnam, from which country I was barred for various reasons, but the interest of the world was focused on Laos, where yet another ceasefire had been proposed and whose capital was to be visited both by Kissinger and Agnew. Until the peace treaty was signed the Americans were continuing and even increasing the bombing raids by immense B-52 planes, whose crimson trails could be seen at dusk from the bar of the Million Elephant Hotel. The man responsible for this murderous policy was the then US Ambassador in Vientiane, G. M. Godley, known to fellow diplomats as Almighty Godley. During one invasion of the Plain of Jars, Godley was asked if he had any difficulty living with a job that required him so often to make decisions involving the lives and deaths of thousands of people. 'Hell, no,' Godley replied, 'I'm having a marvellous time.' He had picked his team from men who spoke French, had no family ties and were not, in his own phrase 'yellow'. This explained why so many of Godley's associates had served with him in the Congo, including some top CIA agents and one attaché, responsible for the press, who is said to have captained a submarine in the Polish Navy.

It cannot be said that Vientiane was agog for Agnew's visit. There was more gossip concerning a Russian spy who had wrapped his car round a tree, winning the newspaper headline 'Drunk Diplomat Fired'; or concerning the sexual exploits of a compatriot of mine, who appeared to be very excited by the Mekong. 'I was passing by one night,' said an Australian friend, 'and I saw this group of Laotians peering down into the river. It was this Englishman, screwing an American air hostess. And this was the rainy season!' An American lady asked a group of us journalists if it wasn't exciting to be in Laos at this historic time, but nobody answered because, as usual, it seemed like a time of dreams. One day my eye was caught by a *Bangkok Post* headline, 'Reds Launch Big Drive In Laos', but it took me at least five seconds to realise that this was the country in which I was standing. However I thought I should inquire about this Red drive and about politics in general, so I made an appointment to meet a diplomat in an embassy on the far side of town. When the time came I took a taxi, whose driver was accompanied by a lady, and we set off in what I assumed was the direction of the embassy. After a time the houses thinned out and we came into open country, for all I knew Pathet Lao country. I asked the driver to stop, whereupon he smiled, pointed towards the woman and then to some bushes to indicate that I might enjoy her favours. How can one work in such a country? It was only by exercise of all reserves of my will-power that I got out to the airport for the arrival of Vice-President Agnew.

There were signs of his approach even before I left the Constellation, whose balcony had an armed guard overlooking the route, and whose café was filled with Russian and North Vietnamese air passengers whose onward flight to Hanoi from Moscow had been held up by the preparations for Agnew. However there were no crowds lining the route or anyone at the airport except security men and the press. We had been penned into a rope compound where I met the former Polish submarine captain and joined in the general mirth at the news we had just heard over the radio that Nixon was a candidate for that year's Nobel Peace Prize. The Aeroflot plane was at one end of the runway next to a huge American transport craft which had arrived the previous day bringing Agnew's bullet-proof car. The vehicle was now parked and ready to drive to the steps of Agnew's Vice-Presidential jet. A great many American security guards in white shirts and black ties were walking about the airport talking into their walkie-talkie sets, and I imagine that some sort of military sweep must have been made of the area within rocket range. When Agnew's enormous plane landed and the enormous Agnew got out and stepped into his enormous car, the very enormity of it all only emphasised the pettiness of the occasion. Why was this tiny country being visited by this third-rate man from the country that was bombing it? Did the brain in the Vice-President's big, handsome head really think it was making history, or did it dream back during the speeches and ceremonies to political squabbles in Baltimore, to property deals and tax swindles? Perhaps history will never know, or care. At any rate, a ceasefire agreement for Laos was signed.

In December the same year, 1973, I was again at Vientiane airport and watched two Russian transport planes unloading some trucks and about a platoon of Pathet Lao troops wearing baggy, grasshopper-green fatigues and caps of a design that was fashionable for women in England about five years ago. The Pathet Lao troops are allowed by the peace treaty to move quite freely about Vientiane, to shop at the morning market and make their propaganda. The increasing Communist presence is noticeable at the Constellation Hotel, which carries a tourist poster for Lake Baikal—'the blue gem of Siberia'. In contrast to Cambodia, where there was no peace and to South Vietnam, where the peace was continually broken, both sides in Laos seemed anxious to make the peace work. They even credit each other with peaceable intentions. The unloved US Ambassador Godley had gone, and I read with delight that Congress had turned down his appointment as chief US adviser on East Asia.

On this trip I went for three days to Luang Prabang, the royal capital, which I had not been to before on the grounds that one needed a permit, but in fact because I was too drowsy to leave Vientiane. It lies on the Mekong about 250 miles away by boat and 150 by air. The Pathet Lao territory begins about 15 miles further upstream but there were still a few signs of war even closer. In the weeks before I was there three men had been killed in an ambush four miles to the south, a grenade had been thrown into a cinema, and a bullet pierced the cockpit of one of the Royal Air Lao passenger planes. Such incidents are expected in violent, political towns like Saigon, Jerusalem or Belfast, but seem unnatural in Luang Prabang, in spite of many years of war. Most of the town lies on a high spit of land between the Mekong and one of its tributaries, which here flow between heavily wooded forests. From either side of the long central road you look down on powerful brown streams, dotted with long-boats and fishing buoys and, in the shallows, women washing and children playing about with old lorry tyres. The houses are well built in wood and the pagodas have finer carvings and richer gold leaf than anywhere else I have been in a Buddhist country. As early as four in the morning you hear the irregular beat of pagoda drums and then of the gongs, which are somehow more soothing than sleep itself. At this time of the year it was very cold in the early morning so that the tri-shaw drivers outside the market were wearing leather jackets and caps, and stamping their feet as they waited. There was a smell of wood smoke and morning mist, which cleared by nine into a sky of perfect blue, by which time it was warm enough to sit at an outside café, drinking freshly pressed pineapple, lemon and orange juice. People are friendly except that this was the only place in Indo-China where I had seen children with catapults—dozens of them— and sometimes trained on tourists who climb up the hill to the king's pagoda.

Otherwise, as a drinking companion said, Luang Prabang is the last paradise. 'The people,' he went on, 'are peaceful, polite and friendly, even after all they've been through. But it's changed a bit from the time you could leave your house unlocked or leave your motorbike in the street if you were too drunk to drive. I've really enjoyed it here.' I asked him where he was from, assuming Vientiane, but he said: 'I am Cambodian from Phnom Penh, but I've been working here ten years. Every year I've gone back to Phnom Penh for a holiday and I used to enjoy a whole fortnight. But now I can't stand more than three days. Our flat is full of relatives from the country who are refugees and have lost everything and are very unhappy because so many are dead. They cry all the time. It makes me very depressed. Ah yes, *monsieur*, Cambodia was a paradise once but now one has to come to Luang Prabang. It is the last paradise left.'

Part Six
SAIGON AGAIN

1

I quote from a frivolous novel, *Christiane de Saigon*: 'From six to eight before dinner at the corner of the Place du Theâtre and the admirable Rue Catinat, the Continental—bordering the pavement—is at once a club, a salon, a stock exchange and a station. Elsewhere there are real clubs and salons but it is here you get the gossip and the business deals, romances and money, the news from Europe and Asia. I know old Frenchmen in Indo-China who have never been to Hue, Phnom Penh or Hanoi but there is not a white man from Tonkin, Cambodia, Laos or even China and Japan, who is not bound to know Saigon and through Saigon, the Continental.'

This novel by Louis Roubaud was published in 1931 and its plot revolves round the scandal that had convulsed Saigon over the decision by the Governor to expel white prostitutes. It was the main debate for years at the Continental Hotel. The subject of argument has now changed but the Continental continues, and one could almost write the history of the country around this famous café. Physically little has changed in this three-storey, white stucco building with its restaurant and its café open to the street under an L-shaped colonnade. The elegant Rue Catinat, which was out of bounds to French other-ranks during the late Forties and early Fifties, has been renamed Tu Do and is now not so elegant; the theatre has been turned into a parliament without any loss of histrionics; a skyscraper hotel, the Caravelle, has been built facing the Continental across the square. The real changes that have occurred are in the clientele of the café.

Even in the days of *Christiane de Saigon* there were patrons of the Continental who worried about Vietnam and political problems. A left-wing journalist, Andrée Viollis, stayed at the Continental during part of a fact-finding inquiry into repression through the colony. In her resulting book, *Indochine S.O.S.* (1932) she accused the French army of two massacres, both resulting in the death of more than a hundred people (and one of them close to My Lai), of torture and exploitation. Then as now, part of the Mekong Delta was under the influence of the Communists, whose leaders agreed to meet Mlle. Viollis on a street corner in Saigon. 'Excuse us for not coming to your hotel,' they told her, 'but the *boys* (waiters) are almost all spies. If they saw us with you we'd risk being arrested.'

The Continental survived the Second World War and the Japanese occupation, although it lay on the flight path used by allied bombers in the attacks on Saigon. The hotel suffered more during the civil war against the Viet Minh, the precursors of the Viet Cong, who regarded its open café as a tempting target for bomb attacks. Early in 1954 the British writer Norman Lewis arrived in Saigon, checked in at the Continental and after a wash went to look out of his window. At that moment he heard a colossal explosion and saw below him dead bodies and wounded men clutching on to each other like Greek dancers. In Graham Greene's novel it is *The Quiet American* himself, Alden Pyle, who has contrived the explosion in order to win support for a Third Force which then, as still today, was seen by some elements of the secret services as the only hope for Vietnam. It had been in the Continental that Pyle first met Phuong, the Vietnamese girl whom he takes away from Fowler the English journalist: 'It was the early evening, in the momentary cool which came when the sun had just gone down, and the candles were lit on the stalls in the side streets. The dice rattled on the tables where the French were playing Quatre Vingt-et-un and the girls in the white silk trousers bicycled home down the rue Catinat'.

The ranting American journalists whom Greene so despised were still very evident at the Continental when I first went there in 1966, except that now they wore uniforms, boots, even bandages. There was one group of photographers, some of them British and most of them now dead, who seemed to be always drunk on gin, marijuana and danger. Besides the journalists, there were a few famous writers, like John Steinbeck, who went about heavily armed, to the distress of his military escorts. Before going to sleep at night, John and Mrs Steinbeck would practise taking cover behind the bed in case of a mortar attack.

The view from the Continental café was marred in late 1966 by a grotesque statue showing two soldiers advancing upon the Parliament with sub-machine guns and faces of great savagery. This statue displeased above all the proprietor of the hotel, Philippe Franchini, a Corsican Vietnamese and a well known painter—although the exhibition of his I saw at the Continental was rather macabre for my tastes. The paintings, etchings and montages—*Terres d'amour, nuits de mort*—included studies of parted vaginas, impaled corpses, pink baby dolls behind prison bars, and a naked, whimpering girl with her bottom stuck in the air—a work that was marked as sold to the deputy manager of the Caravelle Hotel. I have not seen M. Franchini's films, one of which had the unique distinction of being banned by the first Paris Banned Film Festival, but he denied to me that he once wanted to make a film of fifty Japanese eating spaghetti. He is over-modest about his hotel, which he once claimed had the worst food, the rudest staff and the ugliest prostitutes in the east. In fact the staff are polite.

The Continental Café, being open to the street, has always been a favourite for pedlars, especially cigarette girls, who fight loudly for custom among themselves. The most distinguished-looking are the fortune-tellers and the most unpleasant, on no account to be paid, are the women collecting money for spurious charities. The Continental has always demanded propriety from its customers, except from the crazed

General D, who was governor of a military region until being persuaded by some branch of the CIA to lead a third force in a military coup. Torture is blamed by some for his curious habit of turning up at the Continental to lecture the customers in Vietnamese, French and English, none of them comprehensible. Apparently he is against sexual vice, for I have seen him grab a prostitute and throw her into the street. And undoubtedly he dislikes the politicians. He got so excited once by the sight of senators going by that he ran out of the café, stopped in front of the Parliament, and pulled out his sexual member to show his contempt for that assembly.

In 1971 I found the Continental had changed. There had always been one or two men there in drag—the rue Catinat was famed for this even in Graham Greene's time—but now it had become what the Americans call a gay bar—at least after eight o'clock in the evening. The gents would be crowded with twittering Vietnamese young men, some of them dressed as women, discussing their boy friends and playing about with their make-up. On one hilarious occasion the homosexual set arrived in force when the Shriners, a quasi-Masonic body, were holding their annual dinner at the Continental Hotel. The epicene boys, with eye shadow and fluttering hands, gazed adoringly at the huge American engineers wearing unaccustomed suits and fezzes embroidered with names of eastern cities like Cairo, Baghdad and Mecca. The contrast was appropriate for the recent and widespread homosexual cult in Saigon was in part attributable to the presence for so many years of half a million Americans who bought up the local women and mocked the pride and virility of the local men.

I went back to the Continental in 1973 to find that the front tables were occupied by Poles and Hungarians from the International Control Commission, the body intended to safeguard the peace treaty. There were a few homosexuals but more ordinary bar girls, and one American engineer who has been drinking there for at least seven years. In the entrance to the hotel there was a slight commotion. A Vietnamese lady politician had just been banned from holding a cocktail party and now was holding an impromptu conference for the foreign press. In 1973, as in 1931, it is risky to talk to journalists in the Continental, but this lady had just come out of prison and knew what she was doing. She wanted to win support for a Third Force.

2

I could never work up any interest in what are described as politics in Saigon. Elections are rigged with an efficiency that has impressed even the Poles and Hungarians on the peace-keeping commission; almost all the members of the House of Assembly are up for sale to the various feuding generals; indeed sometimes the Saigon newspapers publish the going price of a vote in a big debate. President Thieu's narrow victory in last November's budget debate must have cost many thousands of pounds but this will be amply repaid by new sources of graft to his personal organisation. The real politics of Vietnam is a straight contest between the property-owning ruling class and those who would dispossess them; between the police and the army on one side, and the National Liberation Front on the other. Among the students and the professional classes there may be a few loyal liberals or social democrats but they have no chance of power or even influence. The 'Third Force' advocates who occasionally get their names in the press, largely the foreign press, may be brave individualists, cranks or martyrs, but are most often crooks who want to bump up their price for support in the House of Assembly. If an individual critic annoys the police or the military, his statements will not appear in the press and he may be thrown into prison.

Only religious differences slightly confuse the straight confrontation of right and left. In the early Sixties Buddhists were photographed setting fire to themselves in protest against the tyranny of the Catholic President Diem. Certainly Diem was a religious bigot, but there was also much truth in his argument that the Buddhist revolt was a blind for Communist pressure. The Catholics in South Vietnam are not merely anti-Communist but a largely bourgeois group, with a share of wealth, land and influence disproportionate to their size. Although there are many rich Buddhists, their main following lies in the villages and the poor parts of cities. Their purely religious protests against Diem were given support by crowds whose motive was much more political. The rebel monks at the An Quang pagoda were probably not themselves Communists, as Diem sometimes insisted, but they served the purposes of the Communists, as do all dissident sects.

On the tenth anniversary of the death of Diem, on 2 November 1973, his remaining followers were permitted not only to hold a memorial mass but to turn it into a show of political loyalty. I was curious to attend, for I have long been interested in the argument over the overthrow of Diem, his brother Nhu and the lovely but venomous sister-in-law, Madame Nhu. For some years before and after his fall Diem's name was abhorrent to liberals in America. He was considered a bigot, a recluse who would not listen to counsel except from his brother, the still more tyrannical chief of police, and from Madame Nhu, who gloated in public over the burning monks. Diem and his family were accused of hating Americans and of sabotaging the military and financial help so generously given them by the United States. These criticisms were voiced by most American journalists at the time, in particular by David Halberstam of the *New York Times*.

For his first two years in office President Kennedy refused to change his policy of supporting Diem. He was a fellow-Catholic and his father Joseph Kennedy had been largely responsible for persuading North Vietnam to allow Catholics to leave as refugees to the south. Perhaps Kennedy felt some bond with the rich, aristocratic brothers and sisters who ran Vietnam as a family business. At any rate he grew shrill in

Diem's defence, denounced David Halberstam as a liar and barred the *New York Times* from the White House. But by November 1963 he had come round to the view that Diem must go or South Vietnam would be lost. The handling of the coup was left to the US Ambassador Cabot Lodge, who was most upset when, contrary to his instructions, President Diem and his brother were murdered.

There are many Vietnamese today who regret Diem, not because he was good but because he was not as bad as what followed. Others regret him because his regime, although corrupt, was puritan in its repression of crime and prostitution. I have heard others say that whatever Diem's faults he at least was a strong man with the character of a leader. I have never heard that compliment paid to either Ky or Thieu. Others speak well of Diem because he was killed by the Americans: in Vietnam there is no petty distinction between killing and merely conniving at the coup.

At the memorial mass in Saigon Cathedral, ten years later, there were many bus-loads of mourners, supplemented by youth groups in smocks and cross-garters rather like Morris men, who did the funeral dance with banging of sticks. We were given an English translation of a speech delivered by 'the representatives of the organizing committee for the memorial service of late President Ngo Dinh Diem and his younger brother'—nobody mentioned the name of the much-hated Nhu. 'This memorial service,' the speech claimed, 'is not aimed at rekindling any hatred or exposing the criminal responsibility of anyone whatsoever. Were he living this day, President Diem's magnanimity would not have tolerated such an undertaking.' There was little magnanimity to be found in the Diem supporters with whom I spoke. The secretary of the committee which had arranged the celebratory mass was a severe professor wearing a smart, dark suit and a constant scowl. At every question I asked, he writhed and sighed and hissed with exasperation that I, a foreigner, should question the popular love for his murdered leader. I asked what he thought of the reports that the Emperor Bao Dai, once exiled by Diem, might come back to Saigon and to politics. The Professor's lip curled (literally curled) and his eyes swelled with fury, as he said that Bao Dai was a child, an old spoiled, crying child. I asked if Buddhists were taking part in the memorial tribute to Diem, to which the Professor said: 'Yes, it was not just the Catholics who supported him. This afternoon there will be a memorial service held at a Buddhist pagoda.' I could not resist asking if this was the An Quang pagoda, whose militant monks led the protest by suicide against Diem. The Professor glared at me sideways, hissed and said that the An Quang pagoda had sent them a telegram of condolence. Before I could query this most improbable statement, the professor asked me a question in turn: what role had America played in the coup against Diem? I explained for the third time that I was not an American, and the interview came to an end.

From the cathedral I walked to the main Catholic cemetery, where a Mass was to be said in front of Diem's tomb, which is topped by a hideous, grey, plastic slab. It was a morning of activity at the cemetery, for Diem's anniversary falls on All Souls' Day, when Catholics honour the dead. A memorial service had been held by the French *ancien combattants*, not least of them M. Ottavj, the proprietor of the Royal Hotel, who was secretary of the War Honours Committee. As the Diem supporters proceeded between the graves, they passed M. Ottavj going away in his black suit and tie, with his heavy stick and his no less heavy walk.

In front of Diem's tomb there was a VIP area barricaded by barbed wire of the latest kind—rather like rose thorns—on which I managed to cut my finger. Speeches were made by a politician, the mayor of Saigon and lastly a prelate, who also conducted the mass, as blue smoke shot from the tomb to mark the departed spirit. There was something odd in this ceremony for a man who is still widely disliked in Vietnam,

and some of the British journalists cracked jokes comparing
the whole thing to Ireland. One of us laughed loudly, just at the
wrong moment; it was very wrong, I suppose. After the mass
some young Vietnamese who had been standing in front of us,
turned round and asked bitterly if Diem had been killed by the
Americans. We said we were British, but they refused to hear
and asked us again for an honest reply—did the Americans
murder Diem? So just to please them, we said: 'Yes, of course
we did.'

It was strange to attend a rally in honour of Diem; still
stranger, the following day, to go to a Communist press briefing
at Tan Son Nhut airport. By the terms of the ceasefire agreement, the People's Revolutionary Government (PRG) have
stationed a team of observers in the territory ruled by the
Republic of South Vietnam. The site of the camp may have
been chosen to keep the Communists apart from the people of
Saigon, or to discourage rocket attacks on the airport.
Tan Son Nhut is a dismal place because of the noise from
helicopters and jets, and the landscape of concrete and mud,
yet the Communists, with their discipline and their industry,
have made a tolerable dwelling-place even here. Before this
first visit I had been told (in whispers) by Saigon people
that the VC camp had a vegetable plot. This achievement
impressed people still more because of the contrast with
ARVIN, who steal rather than grow much of their food. The
Communist vegetable garden may be a propaganda ploy, but
was nevertheless impressive, as was the neatly designed camp
with lawns surrounded by stone borders and pathways orna-
mented with vases.

The Saturday press conference starts at nine in the morning
and goes on for about three hours. This length of time is
thought necessary to rebut all the statements made by the
Saigon government during a week of daily press conferences.
Both sides accuse each other of ceasefire violations while the
Communists also accuse Saigon of 'land-grabbing operations'.

The very quantity of these allegations and incidents dulls their impact, at least on myself. 'Last week the Saigon American puppet government committed 743 ceasefire violations, bringing the total to 32,463 ceasefire violations, and 682 land-grabbing operations, bringing the total to 49,583 land-grabbing operations.' There was one moment of interest when the spokesman, a colonel, was asked if it was true that the PRG had blown up a train. 'Yes,' came the reply, 'the train of the Saigon American puppet regime had entered the territory of the PRG and, after careful consideration, we decided to destroy it.'

The spokesmen at these conferences are all from the PRG, that is the South Vietnamese Communists who used to be called Viet Cong; but the North Vietnamese army also sends a liaison officer, who sat next to me during the conference. He was obviously even more bored than I by the catalogue of battles and land-grabbing operations, for when I started to read a book, he started to read one too. I asked what his book was about and he said 'Patriotic poems'. He looked over at my book, *Right Ho, Jeeves*, but luckily did not ask me about its political content. He asked me about the Diem mass on the previous day and I asked him how the North Vietnamese could travel back to Hanoi. 'By American Air Force planes,' he said with a chuckle, 'the very same planes that were bombing us.' He asked me about the rice situation in Saigon and said: 'The Saigon regime is fighting two wars—the Viet Cong War and the Rice War.' Highly pleased with himself, he went on to his next joke which I think he had told many times before: 'Poor Nixon. He has both Watergate and Vietnamisation gate'.

Well, as Bertie Wooster might have remarked in *Right Ho, Jeeves*, I didn't think the joke was a patch on the one about the travelling salesman and the clergyman's daughter. Politeness, however, compelled me to smile. And I later heard that the PRG were vexed with the North Vietnamese and me for talking during the press conference.

3

When I got to Saigon in 1973, I found a letter that had been posted to me in 1971 but had reached the hotel only in 1972. The reason for its delay was explained by a stamped apology on the envelope—'MISSENT TO SOUTH KOREA'. Post office clerks are not the only people who get confused between Vietnam and Korea, two eastern nations divided by politics and a war. The analogy is self-evident and, as Conor Cruise O'Brien once pointed out, when people do not understand a political situation, they try to explain it by an analogy.

Even Dr O'Brien's Ireland has been invoked as an analogy with Vietnam. Marxist and, still more, Catholic politicians have tried to present both countries as victims of 'imperialism'; indeed the fatuous Senator Edward Kennedy (whose family has been much to blame for the Indo-China tragedy) once managed to work Northern Ireland, South Vietnam, Biafra and Bangla Desh into one compound analogy unfavourable to the British. I have heard an IRA man compare his pub-bombers and street snipers to Viet Cong troops, claiming for both a victory over foreign imperialists who, so he maintained, had withdrawn support for the puppet regimes of Faulkner, in Ireland, and Thieu in Vietnam.

The flaws in this analogy are almost too obvious to need mentioning. The mutual involvement between Britain and Ireland, Saxon and Celt, goes back thousands of years and in no way resembles the colonisation of South-East Asia during the last century. Although Roman Catholics play an important role in both countries, in Northern Ireland they side with the

174

rebels, in South Vietnam with the Saigon government; although more than a thousand people have died in the Ulster troubles, mostly by murder or terrorist bombs, this bloodshed does not amount to a civil war, still less to the Vietnam war with its millions of deaths. There were 60,000 deaths in South Vietnam during the first year after the ceasefire of January 1973.

There is one valid analogy between Vietnam and Ireland but it does not appeal either to Marxist or Papal apologists. The English subjection of Ireland during the sixteenth and seventeenth centuries was motivated by fear that this still Catholic island might be used as an invasion base by France or Spain. As late as the Second World War, the British government under Churchill considered invading the Irish Free State to get the use of its ports. The American intervention in Vietnam was also largely inspired by the strategic fear that all South-East Asia would fall into the hands of China.

Although there are no true analogies with Vietnam, it is instructive and sometimes amusing to compare the recent blunder with other American ventures in East Asian affairs. The most dramatic of these was the opening up of Japan in the 1850's to American trade, American concepts of progress and even American sexual habits as symbolised by Lieutenant Pinkerton, seducer of Madam Butterfly. America's next big Asian venture, the conquest of the Philippines, was less neatly accomplished, less justifiable in the history books, and therefore almost unknown to modern Americans.

In the last decade of the nineteenth century both the Philippines and Cuba rose in revolt against Spain. In the Philippines, which had been ruled by fire and the sword for nearly three centuries, the Spanish massacred hundreds of dissidents and in 1896, killed the Filipino writer and patriot leader, Jose Rizal. Filipinos raised a guerilla army and took revenge on the Spaniards, sometimes burning Franciscan friars over slow fires. The revolt was still growing in 1898, when the US battleship *Maine* was blown up in Havana harbour and the

United States went to war with Spain. President McKinley first sent a fleet to capture Manila then raised an army of volunteers whose purpose was not quite clear, since when the Spanish withdrew the Filipino nationalists wanted complete independence. Indeed Commodore Dewey, the US Navy Commander, had gone on record as saying that Filipinos were 'superior in intelligence and more capable of self-government than the Cubans'.

But back in the United States, a combination of interests favoured outright annexation. 'We are a conquering race,' said Senator Albert J. Beveridge. 'We must obey our blood and occupy new markets and, if necessary, new lands.' The head of the Union Theological Seminary claimed that 'whenever on pagan shores the voice of the American missionary is heard, there is fulfilled the manifest destiny of the Christian Republic.' The Secretary of the Treasury said that 'philanthropy and five per cent' could go hand in hand; while the St Louis *Post Dispatch* argued more crudely: 'The Filipino is treacherous and deceitful. Besides we want his country'. These arguments got a forceful backing from Rudyard Kipling, who urged the American people at the beginning of 1899:

> Take up the White Man's burden—
> Send forth the best ye breed—
> Go bind your sons to exile
> to serve your captives' need;
> To wait in heavy harness
> on fluttered folk and wild—
> Your new-caught, sullen peoples,
> Half devil and half child.

The 'expansionists' who wanted to grab the Philippines, were opposed by the 'anti-imperialists' who included millionaires like Andrew Carnegie; labour leaders like Samuel Gompers; writers, like Mark Twain; sugar and hemp growers who feared cheap Filipino competition; Liberal Democrats who stuck up for Filipino rights; and Southern Democrats, who did not want to incorporate 'a mongrel and semi-barbarous population into our body politic—inferior but akin to the Negro.'

On December 10, 1898, at the Spanish-American peace talks in Paris, the Philippines were transferred to US sovereignty but the Filipino Army Commander, Emilio Aguinaldo, held back from a war in the hope that the treaty would not be ratified by the US Senate. However the leading 'expansionists' like Henry Cabot Lodge, Theodore Roosevelt and at last McKinley himself succeeded in pushing the treaty through the Senate. On 4 February a jumpy American sentry in Manila shot and killed a Filipino officer, to set off a war that would last four years and cost 250,000 lives.

The third verse of Kipling's prophetic poem began:

> Take up the White Man's burden—
> The savage wars of peace . . .

. . . and reading the history of the Philippines War one is constantly struck by comparisons with more recent, no less savage events. The Amigos, as Aguinaldo's troops were called, used roughly the same guerilla tactics as 'Charlie'—the Viet Cong. Peasants by day, they took up arms at night to attack outposts, supply routes and villages. They countered American Maxim guns and superior rifles with home-made booby traps such as sharpened bamboo stakes in the path. When a journalist remarked on the Filipino bravery, General Lloyd Wheaton roared: 'Brave! Damn 'em, they won't stand up to be shot at'. The Americans controlled the towns and set up 'friendly' governments in the villages, but the mass of the people were apathetic or sided with the Amigos. Yet American experts told McKinley early on in the war that Aguinaldo represented 'less than half of one per cent of the population.' Then, as later in Vietnam, the Americans faked the casualty lists and drew much comfort from 'captured documents'.

The Amigos, like the Viet Cong, used terror against colla-
borators; the Americans replied in the same fashion. Then, as
in Vietnam, correspondents complained that the Americans
cut off the ears of the dead and tortured their prisoners with the
'water cure'. 'I want no prisoners', General Jake Smith told his
men. 'I wish you to kill and burn; the more you burn and kill
the better it will please me.' A Republican Congressman said
about North Luzon: 'Our soldiers took no prisoners, they kept
no records, they simply swept the country, and wherever and
whenever they could get hold of a Filipino they killed him'.
The anti-Imperialists grieved that the number of bars in Manila
had risen by twenty-fold; that VD accounted for one in four
cases of military illness. Edward Atkinson, an anti-Imperialist
leader, called Manila 'the world's most enormous licensed
brothel', just as Senator Fulbright, sixty years later, called Saigon an 'American brothel'.

After Aguinaldo's capture in 1901, the Filipino resistance
started to sag and the war finally petered out with a few blood-
thirsty incidents in outer islands.

> Take up the White Man's burden—
> The savage wars of peace—
> Fill full the mouth of Famine—
> And bid the sickness cease . . .

Following Kipling's advice, the Americans turned from the war
to what they would now call 'pacification' or 'civic action'.
Soldiers and civilians carried out mass vaccination, introduced
toothbrushes and soap, built schools and staffed them with
English-speaking teachers. Even baseball was introduced
although rich Filipinos altered the rules so that they did not
have to run between bases. A Filipino nationalist in 1925 recalled 'the inspiring spectacle of American soldiers leaving their
guns and, as emissaries of peace and goodwill, with book in
hand, repairing to the public schools to teach Filipino children

the principles of free citizenship', And so, Americans once used to hope, it could have happened in Vietnam.

A young lieutenant who fought in the Philippines went on to become General 'Vinegar Joe' Stilwell, the China hand and Chief US adviser in World War II, who is still blamed by some Americans for the success of Mao Tse Tung. Although Stilwell was a much abler man than the US generals and diplomats in Vietnam, he faced even worse frustrations. Chiang Kai Shek was corrupt; he was more concerned with politics than with beating America's enemy; he inspired less confidence and support than did his rival Communists. From books like Barbara Tuchman's *Stilwell and the American Experience* one sees that in almost every respect Chiang's regime in China was worse than Thieu's in Vietnam. Recruits had to be led in chains to their units where half of them starved to death because the supplies had been stolen. Both Chiang and his wife surpasssed even Diem and his sister in cruelty, clannishness and pig-headedness, without the redeeming virtue of any principle. But unlike the Diems, both Chiang and his wife were masters of public relations and knew how to pose to the US people and press as leaders of Chinese democracy. Oddly enough, Chiang's cleverest publicist (hated by Stilwell) was Joe Alsop, who went on to defend Diem, Ky and Thieu.

During the late Forties the United States failed to support Chiang against the Communists but did provide most of the troops for the UN force fighting for South Korea in the early Fifties. The three-year war was replaced in 1953 by a 'ceasefire' only slightly less violent than the one now pertaining in South Vietnam, thus strengthening the analogy between the two countries. Both Vietnam and Korea are split down the middle along a line of latitude; both of the northern states are ruled by the Communist Party and both of the southern states by a general; in both countries both sides blame one another for the incessant ceasefire breaches. Indeed in Korea, where incidents are only sporadic, the peace-keeping talks are far more malevolent than in Vietnam, where 60,000 people were killed in the first year of 'peace'. When I visited Panmunjon, the site of the talks in Korea, the American leader of the United Nations team yelled insults across the table into the face of his Communist counterpart: 'Slaughterer . . . criminals . . . aggression . . hooligans . . . bestial atrocities . . . your armed bandits . . . your gang . . . you and your thugs . . . goons and gangsters . . . you and your cohorts, like bats who cannot stand the light.' Compared to this meeting (which I was told was exceptionally friendly) both sides in Vietnam are statesmanlike in their mutual complaints.

This contrast may in part be due to differences in the national culture, for both regimes in Vietnam would seem to be gentler, or less harsh, than their counterparts in Korea. General Thieu's secret police, although vicious to prisoners, have not created a gangster state such as that run by General Park's CIA; the North Korean Kim Il Sung, who takes whole-page advertisements of self-praise in *The Times*, is a Stalinist and a demagogue when compared to, say, Ho Chi Minh. There are other, deeper differences between Korea and Vietnam which spoil the usefulness of the analogy.

Between the two world wars, when Korea was ruled by the Japanese, the nationalist resistance was led by right-wingers like Synghman Rhee, later the first South Korean President. It was the Russian Red Army that brought communism to North Korea, where there had till then been few party cells. Between 1945 and the Korean War, Rhee crushed the Communists in the South, so that when the North invaded it met few sympathisers.

In Vietnam, the leaders of the resistance against the Japanese and the French were Communists such as Ho Chi Minh, who is widely revered as the father of his country. The regime in the south, on the other hand, was set up (or imposed) and then defended by the French and later by the Americans. Indeed many Vietnamese leaders, like Ky, fought for years against their compatriots on the side of the French colonialists. Again in contrast to South Korea, there is a strong historic communist movement in South Vietnam, much depleted by war and police oppression, but still capable of producing party workers and fighters.

History does not repeat itself, but much can be learned about Vietnam from *The Peloponnesian War* by Thucydides. The parallel occurred to me first when watching the televised US Senate hearing in 1965. Then last year, in Saigon I re-discovered the book in an outdoor, second-hand bookstall—though not, oddly enough, the highbrow stall where they steal books out of one of the foreign libraries. Re-reading Thucydides, I found that he had himself meant his work to be read as a lesson for posterity: 'The absence of romance in my history will, I fear, detract somewhat from its interest; but if it be judged useful by those inquirers who desire an exact knowledge of the past as an aid to the interpretation of the future, which in the course of human things must resemble if it does not reflect it, I shall be content.'

At the start of the war, Athens (*the USA*) was a slave-owning democracy and naval, commercial power with a wide-ranging alliance of friendly cities and islands (*the rest of the Free World*). They were opposed by Sparta (*Russia and China*) an autocracy with a big, standing army and slightly fewer allies, some of them close to the city of Athens (*Cuba, Chile etc.*). Among the Athenians there were both 'hawks' and 'doves', although they did not label themselves with such vulgar tickets but always debated their case in clear, fluent prose. After the death of the great Athenian, Pericles (*Roosevelt*), the management of the nation fell to wild, even demagogic advisers, who wanted to cow the Spartan allies by burning their towns, murdering hostages and breaking the rules of war (*torture, napalm and 'bombing them back to the stone age'*). Athenian intellectuals, trained in Socratic fashion, protested against such methods and were in turn accused of being Spartan supporters (*soft on communism, long-haired demonstrators*). The harsh faction put much stake on an expedition to Sicily, a remote part of the Mediterranean world but then considered vital to the control of Greek-speaking Italy. The leading advocate of the expedition, Alcibiades (*Kennedy/Johnson*) won his way and led the Athenian army to defeat and disgrace.

Alcibiades said that the cities of Sicily were 'peopled by a motley rabble', about whose fate he felt no concern. He was concerned with the greater debate between Athens and Sparta, just as Americans are concerned with their rivalry with the communist powers. Vietnam, like Sicily thousands of years ago, was just a convenient battlefield on which the major powers could fight. Similarly George Orwell prophesied that in *1984* the super-powers would choose such battlefields where they could joust without risking a big nuclear war. I thought of this early one morning in Saigon after awakening from a nightmare that I was in England during the start of World War Three. I dreamed I heard two explosions, which, so people said, came from nuclear weapons dropped on London and Manchester. In fact what I had heard were old-fashioned rockets that dropped in Saigon and did little damage.

4

A few years ago I heard in Saigon that Norman Mailer, the famous American author, had written a book called *Why Are We In Vietnam?* My first response was the unspoken reply: 'Why aren't *you* in Vietnam?' Looking back over the period of the war and the argument it provoked in the United States, I am amazed at how few American writers or commentators bothered to visit the country about which they professed such concern. This criticism applies not only to those who supported the war but those, like Mailer, who rightly opposed it. There were exceptions, such as John Steinbeck who wrote some newspaper articles, and Mary McCarthy who wrote two reporting books, to which one should add various radical singers and actors, who went to the North and might have gone to the South had they been given visas. The American press corps also included a number of good journalists such as Frances Fitzgerald, Ward Just and David Halberstam, of whom the last two wrote novels as well as factual books about their experiences.

But where, I repeat, was Norman Mailer, who might have written a novel as memorable and important as Hemingway's book on the Spanish war, in which America played no part? Why did this great human tragedy produce none of those feature films that have been America's best contribution to twentieth century art? I do not suggest that film-makers or writers, least of all Mailer, lacked the physical courage to stay in Vietnam, which was never as dangerous as Spain, for example. The argument that Vietnam was so publicised by TV that

183

nobody needed to go there was amply disproved by the film of *The Green Berets*, which was shot in America, and was awful. The one very good novel about the country, *The Quiet American*, owes its force and indeed its existence to Greene's having lived there for months on end.

How then explain the failure of Vietnam to stir the American imagination? Thoughtful Americans, when one poses the question, say that their sorrow or guilt concerning the war had inspired a rejection or even dislike of the people and its inhabitants. This explanation yet does not explain why the same country that so disgusted Americans should have intrigued and even delighted other westerners, above all the French, who have just as much reason for guilt because of their role in Indo-China.

Nor can it be argued that cultural differences make the Vietnamese a remote or inscrutable people such as, for instance, the Japanese. The Vietnamese are reserved, even among themselves, but they are tolerant, even friendly to foreigners, and quite ready to share a joke or an argument. Like the Thais and the Burmese, whom they resemble in race and culture, the Vietnamese are far more friendly to foreigners than are the Chinese. Again, much has been made of physical differences, epitomised by the foyer of Saigon's new cinema, whose ceiling is so low that anyone over six foot tall has to stoop. Yet I never sensed that the Vietnamese felt put down or embarrassed because of their small stature.

The lasting friendship and sympathy between French and Vietnamese is interesting to compare with the position of the Americans. Many thousands of Vietnamese live and are accepted in France, a country notably hostile to other minorities like the Arabs, Jews and Italians. And in Vietnam the French tradition has kept alive in spite of the years of Americanisation. The French cultural centres at Saigon and Danang attract just as many students as their American rivals. At Can Tho University, students can now learn French from the latest 'audio-visual' instruments, while the English faculty has to depend on equipment left by the American army. France is the one power to have kept friendly relations with both warring sides in Vietnam, Laos and Cambodia.

One should not deduce from this that the French, as colonialists, were competent or benevolent. On the contrary, they were gross exploiters and often disgracefully crude in their racial arrogance: at French military briefings during the early Fifties, the spokesman would talk of the Communist troops as '*les jaunes*' (the yellows), an epithet unthinkable to the much more tactful Americans.

Six years ago I remarked that American literature contained no Vietnamese woman of note as a heroine or sex symbol. Already this was not quite true since I forgot Bloody Mary, the ferocious market mammy of James Michener's *South Pacific*. Even now, after millions of young Americans have spent a year or more in that country, there is no popular fantasy of the Vietnamese woman. There have been many books and films intended to glamourise Japanese, Thai, Malay, Chinese and Indian women but none that I know on a Vietnamese. Many Americans who lived with a Vietnamese were killed in action but deaths like these did not result in a tragic romance such as *Love Is A Many Splendoured Thing*. Much of the western world lusted or wept for the unbelievable Suzie Wong, a Hong Kong prostitute, but no heroine has appeared from those hundreds of thousands of Vietnamese girls who sold themselves to Americans.

The Vietnamese these days bear little resentment against the former bar girls or those who stay on in business for visiting sailors and businessmen. In contrast to South Korea, where mixed-blood children are beaten up and nicknamed 'made in the USA*', in South Vietnam the bastards born to American servicemen are accepted and even admired in schools. The

---

* President Synghman Rhee said that all children of mixed blood should be thrown into the sea.

Vietnamese, I repeat, are not xenophobic. However the mothers of these abandoned children find it hard to get married to Vietnamese and still harder to adapt to life without the Americans.

Apart from these bar girls, few Vietnamese women, even those who learned English, adopted American ways. They do not smoke nor drink alcohol; they are sexually chaste; at dances they much prefer old tangos, rumbas or fox trots to one of those indolent writhings now called dance in the United States. Above all Vietnamese women have stuck to their national dress. When *Playboy* magazine wanted a special issue on Asian girls showing representatives of each country naked or semi-naked, the Vietnamese girl appeared in an *ao dai*, clothed to the tip of the neck, the wrists and ankles. And even this lady, the film actress Kieu Chinh, told me afterwards that she was furious at having been shown, even clothed, on the same page as girls in the nude. At a time when hundreds of thousands of Vietnamese girls were prostitutes for Americans, *Playboy* could not persuade one Vietnamese actress, model or secretary to pose naked. So conservative are the Vietnamese in their dress, that a proposal to lower the *ao dai* neckline by even an inch causes an argument comparable to that in the West over the topless swim-suit. It was Madame Nhu, oddly because she was puritan, who decreed that the neck should be lowered from chin to collar-bone. The argument still continues, and each year fashion decrees an inch or so change, but there is no talk of changing from Vietnamese to western dress.

Americans used to say that Vietnamese women were mercenary and commercially minded; certainly of the two I knew best, one had the concession for selling tinned crab to the army, while the other used to lie back after making love to tell me about her transport and money-lending business. American men who admire and want to be business executives, cannot accept that, in Vietnam, money affairs are left to women, while men go into the civil service, the army and the professions.

Vietnamese women, just like American men, are business-minded but not necessarily greedy.

Vietnamese women are unsentimental; they do not whisper sweet nothings. Nor are they, like the Americans, obsessed and anxious about the act of sex. They can be downright about their physical feelings sometimes to the point of bawdiness—but they are also romantic about their lovers. One girl I knew, who had fallen in love with an officer, told me she used to be whipped by her relatives because she would not marry the rich man they chose. The next time I met her, when she had married her officer, this romantic young lady gave me a very earthy account of how much she enjoyed being in bed with her husband. This mixture of earthiness and romanticism comes out in some old letters I have from a girl explaining how she wanted a co-habitation licence in order to lose her virginity before she or I was killed in the war. I declined this offer in what I hope was a tactful way but I later learned that she had been killed in one of the accidents that are common in Vietnam.

The Americans in Vietnam were obsessed with castration dread: not the psychological phobia but the actual fear that their girl friend might castrate them. I have heard it said by one American husband that he went to bed each night in terror of losing his genitals. I have never read or heard of an actual case of this happening to an American, but the castration cult does exist in Vietnam. 'Ne nearly loses "It"' was the famous *Vietnam Guardian* headline over the story about a woman who just failed to sever a lover's member. One respectable Saigon housewife has told me (rather too often) the fearful tale of a 'woman who took a knife and went to her husband when he slept and cut off his sexual organs. As he woke up roaring with pain and staggered towards the door, she continued pricking him with the knife so that he died a lingering death. In court she defended herself by saying that his behaviour over the last few years had been a slow death to her.'

Any man is bound to feel uneasy on hearing a story like

that; still more so an American with his cult of the orgasm, his psychological worries and latent dread of women.

One night in Saigon I was feeling depressed after two days at the heroin clinics described in part one. When the curfew descended I made my way to the skyscraper bar with a licence till one in the morning. I ordered a beer, looked round at the bar girls (who knew me of old as a 'cheap charlie' who would not buy them a drink) and prepared to brood for a half hour alone. A new girl appeared and started a conversation: 'I spend one year at college. I know many English words that other bar girls they no know. Do you know word "castration", to rip the flesh from the body? I have very nice apartment. Maybe you come there for fornication and copulation?'

No, not tonight, I said, I was feeling too tired and anyway (joking) I was getting too old for that kind of thing. 'Oh, yes', she replied in her little American accent, 'you old, but I think you very sexy senior citizen.' I reflected, not for the first time, that I had been in Saigon too long.

5

This book on Vietnam ends as the previous one began, with an account of the Saigon Royal Hotel and its proprietor Jean Ottavj. The hotel itself, which was never one of the top establishments in the city, has aged markedly over the last eight years. The rats that always infested it have now multiplied and succeeded in gnawing a hole in the bar so that they brush past the legs of drinkers sitting on the bar-stools. One guest last year was perturbed to find a dead rat with its head cut off outside his bedroom door. The electrical wiring system, that would deserve a place in any museum of technology, has grown still more feeble. The thick cable that runs from the main to the kitchen now has to be propped up with logs of wood and it frequently gives off dull blue flashes of fire. The gramophone, that once used to play sad Vietnamese and French songs, has broken down and is now used only to store lemons for *citron pressé*. The *maître d'hotel*, the *boys* and *boyesses* are loyal and courteous still, but not quite so quick with supplies of fresh towels, Chinese soup or bottles of '33' beer.

The few Royal Hotel patrons, many of whom were British journalists, stood these inadequacies because of their great affection for the proprietor M. Ottavj, who died during Tet in January this year. The news came as no surprise, for in all the years I have known him, M. Ottavj was always frail and frequently bed-ridden; and yet the peaceful death of this very old man has saddened me more than the violent deaths of many younger people. He was a close personal friend, always understanding and sympathetic during the many bad periods, both professional and emotional, through which I have passed in Vietnam. The longer I knew M. Ottavj, the more I grew fond of him and the more I grew to admire him for his courage and sense of honour. I learned from him much about life as well as about Vietnam.

M. Ottavj was short in stature and towards the end of his life he could walk only with difficulty and the use of a stick; but he held himself straight and gave an impression of dignity and authority. Violent and burly American drunks would leave the hotel quietly after a few words (in French that they did not understand) from a man they could have knocked down with a finger. Once a Korean major dragged into the restaurant a confidence trickster, at whom he pointed a pistol, meanwhile ordering food and drink for himself. The military police were afraid to interfere in this argument but M. Ottavj approached the Korean, bade him good day and persuaded him to release the little swindler.

M. Ottavj had excellent and punctilious manners. Every morning at ten and every evening at half past five he would limp downstairs to shake hands with the guests and to inquire after their health, the news and the gossip. He suffered in silence from well-meaning Americans who squeezed his rheumatic hand and addressed him as Jean (pronounced Gene) having seen his Christian name on the hotel menu. I never heard anyone else call M. Ottavj 'Jean' and I never heard him call anyone by a Christian name. In my case this was unfortunate since he stumbled over my surname, which emerged as the polysyllabic 'M. Ou-ou-est'.

M. Ottavj always wore a long-sleeved white shirt, a faded tie, baggy black trousers and sometimes a jacket, for special occasions such as a dinner party, a mass or a memorial to the dead. 'As a rule,' M. Ottavj used to say, 'I hate going to ceremonies, *Mais pour les morts . . .*' M. Ottavj greatly honoured the dead. Once a year, on the Buddhist Day of Departed Spirits, M. Ottavj invited his staff to a sumptuous meal, leaving one chair free for the souls of the dead. In 1968 an English journalist, who was celebrating his safe escape from a most unpleasant battle, came wobbling up to the table and plumped himself down in the vacant chair of the Spirits. It was typical of M. Ottavj's tact that he managed to get the journalist out of the chair and into another without offending either him or the superstitious staff.

M. Ottavj's eyes never lost their dark glow of intelligence but his age could be seen in the mass of wrinkles that made his face look like the contour map of a mountainous region. His lower lip had a permanent swelling, as happens to trumpet players, but in M. Ottavj's case this was attributable to the opium pipe. When I first came to Saigon, M. Ottavj would take me to an opium den but later he had the pipes prepared in his room by a *boyesse*, a lizard-eyed woman who squatted upon his bed. As long as I knew M. Ottavj, he used to complain of inferior opium, adulterated with rubbish, that was all one could get those days in Saigon. 'Ah, M. West, you should have savoured the true opium, the opium of Laos and India. If I could go to Laos now, and smoke some of the real stuff, my illness would disappear.' We offered to take him to Laos but he would not hear of it, having never been on an aeroplane in his life. Through a friend, I obtained some good quality opium for M. Ottavj; but then the friend's go-between moved and M. Ottavj was once again disappointed. He tried morphine and almost killed himself. He tried but did not enjoy marijuana, which made him tipsy. Opium eased the pain in his limbs and freed his imagination to wander among the memories of his eventful life, his favourite books and superstitions.

M. Ottavj was born about 1897 in a village up in the mountains above Ajaccio. He and an old lawyer friend (who came to Saigon even earlier) used to argue for hours about which of their villages had the deeper and richer wells. Neither man had seen Corsica for at least forty years. M. Ottavj said little about his childhood except that he rode horseback and managed the farm in 1914 when the rest of the men were called up for the war. Soon M. Ottavj, too, was called up and served on the Western Front, where he was many times wounded and decorated. He met British troops from whom he acquired a taste for Virginia cigarettes and a knowledge of 'Tipperary', which he sang at a party late last year. After the war M. Ottavj stayed on in the army and served first in Senegal then in Syria, where he saw much action. About 1928 he went to Vietnam where he did two more years in the army before being demobilised at My Tho. 'Ah, M. West', he would say, 'I came here for two years and stayed forty. The Orient draws one . . .' The ex-sergeant went to Phnom Penh as a resident white hunter at the most expensive hotel and then from Cambodia he returned to Saigon and a job as manager at the Majestic Hotel by the river. It was a smart establishment, where every day the guests sat down to a lunch of eleven courses, and each afternoon joined in a *thé dansant* and an *aperitif dansant*, and sometimes a ball in the evening as well. '*Tout Saigon était là, M. West, les femmes en tenue de soir et les messieurs en smoking.*' (All Saigon was there, the women in evening dress and the men in dinner jackets.) The music for the Majestic, as for Schomberg's hotel in Conrad's *Victory*, came from an English all-girl band, in this case under the leadership of one Edna Barrett.

When France fell in 1940, the Japanese moved into Indo-China, billeting many of their officers in the Majestic Hotel. M. Ottavj, who was a Gaullist, decided to leave for the Hotel des Nations, which included the present Royal. He was thrown into prison by the Japanese, who suspected him of having hidden some guns, and he found to his dismay that the hotel lay on the flight path of allied planes attacking Saigon. 'One bomb hit the Opera House and the whole building shook' (here M. Ottavj shook) 'while another hit the former British Consulate killing six senior Japanese who were at dinner. Unfortunately one of the same stick of bombs fell on the Grand Hospital.' In March 1945 the Japanese interned most of the

French, some in the Hotel des Nations where they were crammed six to a room.

In August the same year, the British arrived and the Communists started to agitate for an end to French colonialism. The British tried to suppress the Communists, armed Japanese prisoners and released the Vichy French. After the French had massacred some of the Communists in the Town Hall a mob plundered the French suburb of Roux, killing and wounding dozens of people. 'The Vietnamese women drank the blood of the French,' M. Ottavj used to assure me, whispering so he was not overheard by his Vietnamese second wife.

Anarchy stalked the city and M. Ottavj's hotel: 'One night I was in my room when my dog growled' (here M. Ottavj growled) 'and I fired my revolver. The man in the window fell five metres but when I looked down he had gone. Another time a burglar who had stolen a pile of linen was escaping along the wainscot. I fired twice but he kept running towards me and fell into the road. The police came and took him to hospital where they found that he'd been shot through the chest but was still holding the linen.'

By the late Forties Viet Minh bomb attacks and assassinations had made life difficult for the Saigon hotelier. One of M. Ottavj's regular guests and partner at cards was a French major who was apparently very hirsute and used to hire a Vietnamese barber to come in each week and shave his torso. One day M. Ottavj heard terrible screams, saw the barber run out of the building, then went upstairs to find this friend 'clutching his tripes' and dying. The barber, a Viet Minh agent, had drawn his razor across the major's belly. M. Ottavj's only son was killed at about this time when a mortar attack was launched on an estate in Tay Ninh. According to M. Ottavj: 'When the first mortar fell my son ran out of the building to take shelter, then realised that his girl friend was still inside. He went back to fetch her just as the house received a direct hit.'

M. Ottavj accepted this and other tragedies with the philosophy he had made himself out of the Bible, certain histories of old Egypt, Thucydides and above all Nostradamus, the French medieval astrologer who prophesied that Paris would be destroyed by fire at the end of the twentieth century. M. Ottavj used to explain all world events, from the First World War to '*Hitler et compagnie*', through his study of these pages. '*Nostradamus a tout prévu*', he would say to me during the battles of 1968. 'He said that in the twentieth century a mighty country would be overthrown by a small country. *C'est le Vietnam, M. West.*' His friends used to laugh at these prophecies until October last year, when M. Ottavj forecast the Arab-Israel war, only three days before its outbreak.

In politics, M. Ottavj was a reactionary ('a bit of a monarchist, perhaps') but in no way was he a racialist or intolerant. He disapproved of United States foreign policy but always excused the behaviour of the Americans in Saigon by saying: 'America has not sent here the cream of the cream.' He was much concerned with the preservation of nature, although he confused the American defoliation programme with locally made anti-mosquito sprays, which he denounced as '*Mytox et compagnie*'. Some guests at the Royal Hotel used to blame M. Ottavj's conservationist views for the superabundance of wild life which ranged from rats and mosquitoes to bats, mice, lizards, cockroaches and giant spiders—one of which became famous and was christened after a Fleet Street editor.

A day or two after Christmas last year M. Ottavj asked me into his dingy office but seemed uncertain about what he wanted to say. For the first time since I had known him he seemed embarrassed. At last he said: 'M. West, I know you will be very depressed by this news but on 1 January I am to be made a Chevalier of the Legion d'Honneur'. Of course he was really pleased and really deserved the honour but perhaps he knew that he was near the end of his life. He had grown gloomy recently and more than usually superstitious. He was alarmed by a box of Laotian matches called '999' which he had seen upside-down and taken for '666', which he said was the sign of the Apocalypse. He thought that 1974 might see the beginning of war between the planets, with Earth coming under attack from '*Jupiter et compagnie*'.

On New Year's Day M. Ottavj gave a small dinner to celebrate the award of the Legion d'Honneur. He brought out his best wines and also old photographs of himself as well as the programme of music by Edna Barrett's all-girl band in the Majestic Hotel in the Thirties. Once again I thought of *Victory* and the concept of victory which recurred during this stay in Vietnam and recurs once more in this book. Both sides have claimed victory from the ceasefire. Victory has been claimed even by some Americans who forget the high hopes they once had for this country. The missionaries in the highlands claim a victory over sin, and their radio programme of hymns is known as the 'Victory Hour'.

At this dinner on New Year's Day I was facing a plaque to the *Vieilles Tiges* (Old Joysticks), the French Air Force old comrades association, who hold their reunions here. Around the plaque there are pictures of four Air Force heroes, including Antoine de Saint-Exupéry, the writer, who died flying for France in the Second World War. Two of his greatest books, *Vol de Nuit* and *Pilote de Guerre* also take as their theme the concept of victory. It is the last word of *Vol de Nuit* and the constant refrain of *Pilote de Guerre*, which recounts the fall of France: 'Defeat . . . Victory . . . Terms I do not know what to make of. One victory exalts, another corrupts. One defeat kills, another brings life. Tell me what seed is lodged in your victory or your defeat, and I will tell you its future'.

Heyst, in Conrad's *Victory*, was defeated because he rejected life. For Saint-Exupéry, the only true victory came from acceptance of life and duty to others. In *Terre des Hommes*, which describes his experiences in the Spanish War and his crash in the Sahara during the Paris to Saigon air race, Saint-

Exupéry wrote:

> To come to man's estate it is not necessary to get oneself
> killed round Madrid, or to fly mail planes or to struggle
> along in the snows out of respect for the dignity of life . . .
> It is only when we become conscious of our part in life,
> however modest, that we shall be happy. Only then will we
> be able to live in peace and die in peace, for only this lends
> meaning to death and life.

When M. Ottavj died at Tet, seven years after the death of
Peter Duval Smith, he had stayed true to the idea of duty. He
had served his family as a son and husband and father, his
country as a soldier, his hotel staff as a manager and his
clientele as a friend. He died undefeated, which is as near as
anybody can get towards victory in Vietnam.

Saigon 1974